The Astrology
of Time Twins

The Astrology of Time Twins

by

Peter Roberts
and
Helen Greengrass

The Pentland Press Limited
Edinburgh · Cambridge · Durham

First published in 1994 by
The Pentland Press Ltd.
1 Hutton Close
South Church
Bishop Auckland
Durham

ISBN 1 85821 120 4

Typeset by Elite Typesetting Techniques, Southampton.
Printed and bound by Antony Rowe Ltd., Chippenham.

Contents

Foreword

Is our life and future destiny in some way linked to the precise time of our birth as astrology has taught for thousands of years? Is it possible that there are other people at the present time who are as much like us as if they were our own biological twin?

At the very moment when research in genetics and genetic engineering seems to be suggesting that everything from genius and sexual preference to the details of personality and future diseases are written into our genes, there is emerging a growing body of evidence that the actual time of our birth may be as important to our future development as our biological inheritance.

In this lucid and exciting book, Peter Roberts, Professor of Systems Science at London's City University and Helen Greengrass, co-founder of 'Mirror Images', take us through the growing body of hard evidence derived from their own and others' well-controlled scientific experiments and come up with some surprising and tantalising observations which cannot be ignored by the larger scientific community.

Whether astrology prompts you to out-and-out scepticism or to whole-hearted belief, this provocative book will challenge your assumptions, engage your attention and stimulate your curiosity about this frontier of knowledge – which is in many senses even more radical and revolutionary in its implications than the current developments in genetic research.

Whilst antagonistic sceptics may feel called upon to seek for weak links in Professor Roberts' evidence and arguments, true-believing astrologers should also be provoked to further thought and reflection by his emphasis on the concept of astrological effects only affecting a select group of what he calls 'star born' types. This conclusion is certainly supported by the Gauquelins' findings that it is only the top professionals who show clearly the planetary effects in a statistically demonstrable form. Roberts' own findings, based on this study of time twins, seems to support this view.

So are astrological effects really only applicable to a select minority of people who subsequently become high achievers in their chosen sphere of activity? The evidence at present certainly seems to point in that direction. However an astrologer would argue that people grow and develop throughout their lives and that astrology is potentially a tool for a greater awareness of one's true Self, and that the more an individual knows about his or her planetary potential the more likely it is that he or she will actualise it. To test such an hypothesis in a convincing way will require a very great deal of careful, well-designed research. Until adequate research of this kind is undertaken it is, in my view, too soon to be drawing more than the most tentative conclusions about the true scope of what we might call: 'the astrological dimension of reality'.

In this respect the reader, in evaluating the evidence in this book, should keep in mind the fact that thoughtful astrological research of the kind herein described is still very much in its infancy. Whilst other areas of scientific research globally receive billions of pounds of support per year from governments and industry, astrological research receives no such funding. Its results are, and have always been, entirely the work of a few dedicated, self-motivated individuals. The great pioneers of the past such as Johannes Kepler, who began the scientific quest for the 'grain of gold' in astrology; Michel and Françoise Gauquelin, who compiled their formidable and unassailable body of statistical evidence for the reality of planetary positions in relation to profession; and John Addey, who developed a larger model for understanding astrological effects; are joined at the present time by the authors of this book and amongst others, Professor Suitbert Ertel in Germany, Dr Fuzeau-Braesch in France, and in Britain Professor Hans Eysenck, Michael O'Neill, Dr Percy Seymour, Professor Alan Smithers and organisations such as Helen Greengrass and Brian Hewitt's 'Mirror Images', the Astrological Association and the Urania Trust.

If such a small band of pioneers can achieve so much with so little, it is reasonable to project that given appropriate human and financial resources astrological research will begin to uncover an even richer web of connections between the cosmos and the individual on the lines suggested by the astrological tradition and the daily experience of thoughtful astrologers. In this respect, despite the lack of hard experimental evidence to date, which Peter Roberts and Helen Greengrass rightly report in this book, I am personally still convinced that, given more sensitive and imaginative tests, confirmation of the reality of Sun-sign typologies, and the signs generally, will be obtained. Likewise I am still of the view that further research will bring convincing evidence for astrology's capacity for forecasting future trends in the lives of individuals and world affairs.

However, true breakthroughs in our understanding of this mysterious universe have rarely been won without great individual effort and sacrifice. Much more is yet required in this area. So finally here I would like to pay tribute to Peter Roberts' boldness and intellectual honesty in undertaking this ground-breaking research. For, sadly, it has to be said that even in our seemingly liberal society it takes real moral and intellectual courage for a leading main stream academic to undertake systematic research in this normally taboo area of knowledge where prejudice and an unthinking ridicule from colleagues is almost guaranteed.

With this book, and his previous eye-opening *Message of Astrology*, Professor Peter Roberts joins that rare breed of scientists who are prepared to follow truth wherever it may lead them regardless. *The Astrology of Time Twins* opens up an important bridge between the seemingly irreconcilable twin perspectives of the ancient astrological wisdom and the prevailing scientific world view. A considered study of this book can only encourage an ever increasing two-way intellectual traffic across this formerly destructive cultural divide and promote further research and a larger perspective of the way in which we as individuals relate to each other and to life as a whole. I wish it well in this noble task.

Charles Harvey, August 1993

Chapter 1

Finding a Time Twin

X is talking about her friend Jan:

'Jan was my pen friend in Holland. Her aunt has always called us "The Twins", thinking that we were born the same day, though, in fact, Jan was born at 10 p.m. on 29 May and I arrived at 2.30 a.m. on 30 May in 1942 – so we are $4\frac{1}{2}$ hours apart.

It was many years since I had seen Jan (that was when she visited her aunt – where I used to play as a child), but over recent years we had started writing occasionally. Last September my holiday plans for Switzerland fell through and as I was planning to go to Kent for a wedding, I jokingly said to my father: "If I'm in Kent, then I'm almost in Holland and I could visit Jan." Three days later a letter arrived out of the blue, saying: "We're only a phone call away if you'd ever like to come and stay" . . . and I did!

From the moment I went inside her front door, there were just so many "coincidences" it was uncanny.

I had put on a green blouse and black trousers, only to find that Jan was dressed in the same way.

I immediately noticed that Jan had the poem "If" by Rudyard Kipling on her lounge wall. I have it on my office wall.

Jan wore new glasses with thin blue "sparkly" frames – just like mine. They were so similar that we got them muddled.

After that I began to look for the similarities and asked Jan what size shoes she took (because I take size 7, which is large for someone of my build). She takes size 7 as well.

We were so intrigued by these likenesses that we started to compare notes and found that:

1

- We both make our own personal Christmas cards for special friends.
- We both own a blue and white figurine of a woman holding a goose.
- We have both had to have treatment for trouble with our hands.
- We both have a nephew in the army.

The list seemed to go on and on.'

Is X deceiving herself? Her aunt had called them 'the twins' and so she would tend to think of herself and Jan in that way. Knowing that they were born close together would make her believe that there was something special about the two of them as a pair – just as if they were real twins born to the same mother.

Each of the items on her list is, in itself, not uncommon. At any one time lots of women are wearing green and black. Thousands of pairs of glasses like the ones she describes have been sold. Making your own Christmas cards is not exceptional.

It is only when you put all these things together that you begin to wonder if this is indeed a remarkable case. The sceptic can dismiss it because 'there is simply no possible reason why two unrelated people should bear any special resemblance owing to the fact that they were born at about the same time'. Those who take the claims of astrology seriously can point to it as a good example of the stars revealing their influence on earthly affairs.

How are we to make up our minds? If this sort of thing were happening all the time, there would be no difficulty. We have got thoroughly used to the idea that so-called identical twins resemble one another so closely that they are difficult to tell apart and have lots of traits in common. Besides, there is a scientific explanation for identical twins. They start with the same genetic endowment and so physically they will develop in parallel as if they were the same person. Of course, if unrelated time twins appeared as similar as real identical twins and were just as common then, by now, we would have found a satisfying 'explanation'!

We could take the time twin phenomenon more seriously if it were found to occur quite often. (It might be thought as rare just because no-one has gone looking for it.) It would also be more convincing if the things that were found in common were themselves in the same class. For example, if time twins always worked in the same jobs, had the same maladies and had similar tastes, interests, hobbies etc., then it would seem less like a collection of coincidences.

. . . Here is another recently discovered case reported in the *Weekly World News:*[1]

Barbara Miliceski and neighbour Susan Cooke share a list of coincidences including the fact that they each have three children with the same names: two boys called Ken and William and a girl named Ann:

• Both born on 7 July 1939.
• Both are blue eyed brunettes with identical moles on their right arms.
• Both fathers died when the girls were eleven years old.
• Both were top students who went to college on full scholarship.
• Both met their husbands in college.
• Both married on the same day, 3 June 1961.
• Both husbands went through medical school.
• Both had their first child in the third year of marriage and a second son two years later.
• Both had daughters at the age of thirty-nine.
• Both bought houses on the same street in the same city at the same time.
• Both divorced their husbands at the age of forty-five.
• Both applied to graduate school to study child psychology.

The media have always been impressed by such stories of coincident lives and some accounts have survived the years to become frequently cited 'evidence' that there exists some similarity in life experiences between persons who share the same birth date.

Some Historical Cases of Time Twins

In 1837 the following appeared in Raphael's *Manual of Astrology:*[2]

In the newspapers of February 1820, the death of a Mr Samuel Hemmings was noticed. It was stated that he had been an ironmonger and prosperous in trade – that he was born on the 4 June 1738, at nearly the same moment as his late majesty George III and in the same parish of St Martin's-in-the-Fields; – that he went into business for himself in October 1760, when his late majesty came to the throne – that he married on (8th September 1761) the same day as the king; and finally, after other events of his life had resembled those which happened to the late king, that he died on Saturday, January 29th 1820 . . . 'on the same day and nearly at the same hour as his late majesty!'

Query: After such an authenticated and luminous instance as the foregoing, where the lives of two individuals, born at the same moment, corresponded in every remarkable particular, even in life and death; can the Astrologer be justly accused of superstition or absurdity, should he pronounce the fates of mankind to be subject to planetary influences? Or can any rational mind, upon mature and sober reflection, attribute the foregoing most pointed agreement in their destinies – to mere chance?

This article written in the 1830s appears to be the first recorded instance of the phenomenon of astrological twins, more commonly referred to as time twins. It is a case repeatedly quoted in various publications as supportive of the notion that time twins share some similar pattern in life, share the same fate and are destined to follow the same path.

Many media articles report the case of Samuel Hemmings and King George III as a factual historical account, along with other surviving legendary 'tales'. Such tales are first reported in Alan Leo's book, *The Key to Your Own Nativity*.[3]

Consider for example the case of the Prince of Wales (King George IV) and the chimney sweep who was ushered into the world on the same day and hour that witnessed the birth of the royalty and who was christened 'Prince George'. The reputation of the Prince of Wales speaks of his vices, his follies and his perjuries. It seems his fellow sweep was not too far behind . . . 'Prince George' became a tallow chandler, a ruler in a sense, with apprentices and coteries. He was known to be gallant, courteous, a spendthrift and a gambler. In his own class he became famous; he kept the best asses and ran the best donkey races of the day. Meanwhile his royal compatriot was working out a similar destiny albeit in the higher classes; while the chimney sweep ran donkeys the Prince of Wales ran blood horses. Both met a sorry end. The chimney sweep became bankrupt and on the day his racing donkeys and ponies were put to the hammer the stud of His Royal Highness, Prince of Wales, was sold by Tattersall's.

The comparison between the lives of royalty and the commoner appear as a common theme. Another case cites the King Umberto I of Italy and a restaurateur also named Umberto. While dining in a small restaurant the King was struck by the physical resemblance between himself and the restaurant proprietor. Both had visible and striking white moustaches. Upon enquiry the King discovered that he and the restaurateur had been born on the same day and about the same time – 10.30 on 14 March 1844, in the town of Turin. Both had married women named Margherita on the same day and each had a son named Vittorio. Both the King and Umberto had received medals for bravery.

The King, much struck by these revelations, invited Umberto to attend a shooting match the following day. However, poor Umberto accidentally shot himself while cleaning his gun in preparation. The King expressing a desire to attend the funeral and making whatever were the necessary enquiries, at the time was himself shot and killed by an assassin.

Attempts have been made to validate the sources of these stories.[4] While there does seem to be some evidence to support the Samuel Hemmings case first cited, efforts have not so far validated the Prince of Wales and the chimney sweep. It is likely that story has appeared from fanciful legend and astrological folklore.

One reference which appears not to have been investigated is mentioned in John Harvey's book *The Plantagenents*.[5] This concerns the birth of King Richard I – the 'Lionheart'. He was born at Oxford on 8 September 1157 and placed to nurse with a woman of St. Albans whose son had been born the same night. This foster-brother of Richard's became one of the greatest scientists of his time – Alexander Neckham, encyclopaedist and student of magnetism. The surpassing fame of these two men goes far to support the main contention of astrology, that men's lives and characters are affected by the positions of the stars and planets at birth.

The more astute might enquire: 'But what of all the other babies born at "around" the same time on the night of 8 September 1157? Did all become famous and noteworthy?' . . .

Surviving texts regarding astrological twins seem to centre on one theme – that of royalty and the 'commoner'. Yet it is obvious, is it not, that whatever the astrological indications at birth, the life for a royal will be, by matter of birthright, quite different from that of the common man. Experiences, opportunities and advantages offer a vastly different life experience despite any apparent coincidences. One of the outstanding dissimilarities is the obvious parentage and society privilege of the royal over the commoner.

The lives of lesser known people, with no 'fame' attached and who are born into a similar culture and environment, may indicate a greater 'similarity' in life and many examples have been reported in the media.

On 22 February 1985 in Chicago's Memorial Hospital two babies were born. Each child was given the same Christian names and surname – David Charles Heyman. The families had never met and were not related. The boys' names had been chosen for the same reason: 'David' simply because both families liked the name and 'Charles' in homage to each of the newborn's great grandfather. To add to the coincidences the mothers' respective obstetricians were Dr (Michael) Halpern and Dr (William) Alpern. The two sets of proud parents, both Jewish, inadvertently arranged to have their sons circumcised on the same day by the same *mohel*.[6]

Coincidences aside, it would be quite biased *not* to consider the alternative premise – that time twins show no similarity in life path. These stories are more likely to be gleaned from astrological literature where crude attempts to substantiate the premise of time twins has failed. In the late 1960s Reinhold Ebertin in an article entitled '*Zwei Geburten in der gleichen Minute*' (Two births in the same minute)[7] focuses on two girls of different parentage, Herta and Renate, born in the same minute in the same hospital in 1946. The astrological horoscope would be virtually identical, yet beyond an elementary physical likeness there was little similarity in character or life manifestation. Herta, sexually attractive, pretty and sympathetic, married at the age of twenty-one and had a child six months later. Renate, earnest and ambitious, taught in a special school and remained single and childless. Ebertin concludes that simultaneous birth does not necessarily entail a correspondence in the course of life.

Ebertin may have reached this conclusion after having studied only one incidence of time twins but that is less than likely, since Ebertin's contribution to the world of astrological observations has been his immense study and subsequent publication of many books in the astrological technique known as Midpoints.[8]

Despite the stories which parallel the lives of royalty and the common man, for example, Samuel Hemmings and George I, detailed examination of their life comparisons is bound to reveal discrepancies. Factors such as heredity and environment should not be ignored as powerful influences upon the course of a person's life style and opportunities.

An examination of case studies involving 'popular media' will provide an ample number of examples which reveal amazing similarities. Astrological literature likewise is keen to show similarities so as to support the essence of astrological teachings, but many of the studies to date relating to time twins remain lacking in method and analysis.

Chapter 2

Astrological Research

Attitude of Astrologers

Astrologers often maintain that astrology is itself as science, but this is to extend the meaning of the term 'science' well beyond that assigned to it by academia. Definitions of science contain references to 'a body of theory' and to 'support from experimental work' or to 'data obtained empirically'. Whereas astrologers can point to a theoretical structure for astrology, they cannot claim support from experimental work. What they often regard as empirically obtained data is essentially 'anecdotal material'. If a professional astrologer has many hundreds of clients and is able to note the degree to which her interpretation of the chart in each case corresponds to the character and life experiences of the client, it might be supposed that the totality of this experience would constitute an empirical base. However, for this work to be empirically sound, it must have been done systematically, with precautions to avoid any tendencies towards 'confirming expectations', avoiding leading questions to the client, and noting all failures of interpretation as well as successes. To apply this style of working consistently requires a practitioner with a somewhat sceptical personality. It has to be said that the vast majority of practising astrologers are far from sceptical in style. Indeed, they are usually enthusiastic believers and will devise 'explanations' to cover any case when the interpretation does not fit as well as expected.

One of the main problems facing anyone trying to be objective about the degree to which an interpretation 'fits' a client, is the willingness of most people to endorse an interpretation, provided that it contains some mildly flattering descriptions. In a famous experiment, Michel Gauquelin[1] offered, through a journal, a free horoscope with interpretation to anyone who applied, giving their birth details, with the requirement that they sent him an assessment of how accurately the interpretation fitted their own personality. A large majority of those who responded indicated that the interpretation was an accurate description of themselves – in spite of the fact that Gauquelin had sent the identical interpretation to each one of them! To add piquancy to this 'experiment' the actual horoscope he had used was that of a convicted notorious criminal.

The same kind of problems face therapists who treat patients and have to decide whether their 'cures' derive from the effectiveness of treatment. It is well established that the expectations of patients can have a powerful effect on their health, and indeed, the expectations of the therapist can also have discernible effects. For these reasons, it has been necessary to lay down the 'double blind' procedure for evaluating the effectiveness of a new drug. The group of patients who participate in the experiment are divided into two by random choice but subject to the proviso that there is 'matching', i.e., one group is not, on average, older or more ailing than the other. Then, the members of one group are given the drug and the members of the other group a placebo (a harmless substance with no therapeutic effects). Neither the researcher nor the patients know the identities of those receiving the drug – hence the term: 'double blind'.

Experiments on allegedly curative methods are not considered adequate if they do not conform with the standards of the double blind procedure. Similarly, one should not give credence to claims by astrologers unless there is evidence accumulated and analysed in ways which avoid personal bias.

Types of Research

1. Matching Tests

Astrologers argue that a horoscope should be considered *in toto* – the whole chart, to correspond to the whole person. Picking out particular features of the chart (reducing it to a collection of items) is to go about it the wrong way. This approach has strong echoes with holistic medicine in which the treatment is designed to heal 'the whole person' – not just to alleviate particular symptoms.

There is nothing esoteric or weird about the contention that considera-tion should be given to 'the whole person' and 'the whole chart'. It seems plausible that we recognise faces by using 'the whole picture' (not by adding up the individual features and deciding that this mix corresponds with some mental library record with the same mix listed). However, this gestalt approach is harder to explain, harder to prove and harder to apply, than if the chart were reduced to individual elements and the person considered to be the sum of the elements.

One method has been devised for testing the accuracy of 'whole chart' astrology. An astrologer attempts to match a character description of a person with his or her chart, where both chart and description have been drawn from a small group of people. Thus, if the descriptions are numbered 1 to 10 and the charts for the same people are lettered A to J, the astrologer would be 100% accurate if she matched 1 with A, 2 with B and so on up to 10 with J. It is not essential to be as good as that in order to demonstrate the power of astrology. Getting half of them right would be impressive. Below are listed the probabilities of getting various numbers of correct pairings. (Apart from the zero case, the probability is for 'that number or more'. Thus the probability of getting 2 or more correct pairs is 0.26. This is the reason why the total of probabilities in the list does not sum to 1.)

Correct pairings	Probability
0	0.37
1	0.63
2	0.26
3	0.08
4	0.02
5	0.004
6	0.0005
7	0.00008
8	0.00001
9 or 10	0.0000003

The chance of getting one right is better than evens and of getting three right is only 11 to 1 against. It is necessary to score at least 4 to be interesting – but if anyone got them all right that would be a one in 4 million chance.

Such tests have been performed a number of times, the most celebrated being those of the American astrologer Vernon Clark.[2] Clark published results which were well above chance level and suggested that, indeed, astrologers can accurately divine character from a horoscope. However, there is a problem if the tester, i.e. the one who selects the individuals to be included in the group, is himself an astrologer, because he will tend to select subjects whose charts do conform with their characters. There is no need to ascribe any fraudulent intention; such special choices could take place quite unwittingly.

In order for the tests to be unbiased the selection of individuals would have to be made by a non-astrologer or, better still, using a random method of selection.

Gauquelin[3] has described a variation of the matching test which he himself set for astrologers to attempt. His variation is to provide twenty horoscopes, ten of which are for individuals with some marked trait and the other ten for individuals with the opposite trait, e.g. ten criminals and ten law abiding persons, ten mentally ill and ten sane etc. The astrologer is required to distinguish the two groups using only the charts. Gauquelin reported that though this test had been performed several times, the astrologers obtained only chance level scores.

It can be stated that tests of astrology making use of the whole chart as a means of identification, where the test design has been such as to avoid the possibility of bias, have not yielded results above chance level.

2. Tests on Collections

Even if a horoscope should be considered in its entirety for a satisfactory interpretation, it might still be possible to discover some astrological factor which is common to a collection of subjects, all of whom are similar in some defined way. For example, they could all be red-haired or all be chartered accountants or all have committed suicide.

Many experiments have been carried out using collections of subjects and seeking a common astrological factor. Dean[4] lists an amazing variety of such experiments – over sixty collections, including musicians, clergymen, doctors, bankers, soldiers, idiots, politicians, boxers, psychiatrists and businessmen. The number in each collection was usually in the thousands and for a few collections, over ten thousand. Because it is much easier to obtain the day of birth rather than the time of birth, such tests have concentrated on discovering any unusual sign occupancy of the Sun. The Sun is in each of the zodiacal signs for about one month, and it is straightforward to list the Sun sign for each subject in a collection, given only the birthdate. (It is necessary to know the birth year as well as the day and month because the precise day of the month when the Sun changes sign is not the same every year. The reason for this lies in the fact that the number of days in the year is not 365 but 365¼. We correct for the ¼ by inserting a leap day every four years as 29 February so the calendar is, most of the time, slightly adrift from the Sun's position in the signs – and by varying amounts.)

Despite the many attempts to demonstrate that Sun sign is a significant astrological factor, the results of these labours have been disappointing. One or two of the experiments have a single sign with a statistically high occupancy but that could be expected if this sort of experiment is carried out many times – simply because there are more opportunities for the unexpected to occur by chance.

The striking exception to this litany of failure is the work of Michel Gauquelin. He experimented on the same lines as has been described above but soon abandoned that route and concentrated on the diurnal positions of the planets. In the same way that the Sun appears on the horizon every morning, crosses the sky and sets in the evening, so each of the planets follows this same path, rising and setting. We are not aware of this happening when a planet is in the sky during the daytime because its reflected light is very faint compared with that of the Sun and the planet is effectively invisible. However, if a planet is above the horizon at night it is, in general, clearly visible. Venus and Jupiter are particularly bright compared with the usual stars. The outer planets, Uranus, Neptune and Pluto are not visible to the naked eye.

We can speak of the diurnal position of a planet, meaning where it is on the circle from rising (at the horizon), culminating (at its highest point), setting (sinking below the horizon) and reaching its lowest point (actually out of sight and diametrically opposite its culminating point). Gauquelin studied the positions of the planets in the diurnal circle for his collection of professionals. His collections were unusual in that he sought individuals who were at the peak of their profession. Thus athletes had to be of Olympic calibre; politicians had to be in the national assembly; writers had to be listed in collections of nationally esteemed authors, etc.

Gauquelin's results are remarkable. He discovered that athletes tended to have Mars either rising (just above the horizon) or culminating (just past the highest point). The extent to which this tendency manifested was highly significant statistically. Furthermore, the other collections showed tendencies particular to the profession in each case: thus the prominent planets for each profession are as listed below:

Professional Group	Prominent Planets
Athletes	Mars
Military leaders	Mars and Jupiter

Scientists and physicians	Saturn and Mars
Politicians	Jupiter and Moon
Actors	Jupiter
Writers	Jupiter and Moon

Conversely, there are lower than average frequencies seen in sectors of the circle immediately after rising and after culminating for certain planet and professional group combinations as listed below:

Professional Group	Planets 'Avoided'
Athletes	Moon
Military leaders	Moon
Scientists and physicians	Jupiter
Actors	Saturn
Writers	Mars and Saturn
Painters and musicians	Mars and Saturn

Diagrams illustrating Gauquelin's research findings are given in Appendix 4.

The really interesting point about the Gauquelin results is that they are in close accord with the traditional beliefs concerning the essences of the planets. Traditional teaching has Mars as the planet of energy and conflict (athletes and soldiers), Jupiter as the planet of expansion (actors and politicians), Saturn as the planet of form and structure (scientists) and the Moon symbolising emotion and imagination (writers).

The second area which Gauquelin investigated was that of personality traits. He gauged the personalities of his subjects (the same collections of professionals) from the adjectives used by biographers writing about their subjects. Thus, if a biographer referred to his subject as 'fiery' or 'quick tempered' this would enable Gauquelin to add to his inventory of adjectives associated with planet X (prominent in the chart of this individual). Through a laborious study of biographies the adjectival profile of each of the planets could be constructed. Note that this exercise was independent of the actual profession adopted by a subject. Individuals with Saturn and with Moon prominent can be found even among athletes.

The result of this lengthy procedure was a set of profiles, one for each of the planets. The profiles were in excellent accord with those meanings traditionally attributed to the planets. Below are some adjectives from the lists:

Jupiter	Saturn	Mars	Moon
ambitious	conscientious	active	amiable
conceited	discreet	brave	easy-going
independent	meticulous	dynamic	imaginative
worldly	reserved	reckless	tolerant
.	.	.	.
.	.	.	.

The third area which Gauquelin[5] researched was that of heredity. There has always been a belief that there is a 'family resemblance' among the horoscopes of related people. Actually, this belief does not stand up well to probing by statistical methods, but Gauquelin checked whether parents and their children tended to share prominent planets. Although the effect is more modest than for the deviations from average levels in his collections of professionals, there was a distinct tendency. For example, if a mother has Jupiter rising it is more likely that her son or daughter will have Jupiter either rising or culminating than if she did not. The same applies with equal force to the father – and if both parents have the same planet rising then the chance of their child also sharing it is doubled. The effect was found to be as strong with each of the other planets which had been found in the professionals investigation (Saturn, Mars, Moon and – later on – Venus).

Of great interest, if one is trying to understand the underlying mechanism of astrology, is the discovery Gauquelin made about intervention in the birth process. From his collection of parents and their children he could separate out those where birth had been induced by drugs. This group showed the pattern of prominent planets 'shifted in time' – as though the children had been born earlier than was appropriate astrologically. Moreover, if there were surgical intervention via Caesarian section then the pattern faded altogether (presumably because the actual birth time was separated from the 'appropriate' time by a large interval, the length of which was not constant from birth to birth).

3. *Time Twins*

Yet another form of research in astrology concerns the study of unrelated individuals who were born at nearly the same time and within, say, a hundred miles of one another. The main subject matter of this book is devoted to research in this area, but there have been efforts in the past to argue a case for astrology based on cases of time twins.

Toonder and West[6] list a dozen cases of time twins, including photographs for some of their pairs. They write:

> It would probably be possible to document several hundred such cases from existing records. But to continue listing them would be tiresome, nor would it prove anything from a scientific standpoint. Astrologers, however, insist that the documentation is now sufficiently strong to provoke the interest of the scientifically-minded. Astrologers are confident that large-scale research would prove beyond doubt that cases of 'time twins' are not ascribable to coincidence, and that physical and psychological similarities could be expected to recur.

Charles Harvey, president of the Astrological Association and Dr Frank McGillion carried out an investigation of potential time twins for the television programme 'Brass Tacks'. There had been advertising for people who were born on a particular day and the respondents were invited to attend a studio for the programme transmission. Psychological tests were used to ascertain whether the subjects shared a common personality profile. Occasional physical similarities were noticed and some of the subjects were intrigued to discover extremely like-minded individuals among the company. One of the men in the group, for example, professed to a taste for motor 'scrambling' and also carried out all his own maintenance – which would be unremarkable except that one of the women admitted to the same hobby and she also carried out all her own maintenance. This example is characteristic of the company – an interesting case, but not spectacular. It suggests that really outstanding similarities between time twins are quite rare.

4. *Biological Twins*

Very recently there has been research on fraternal twins which attempts to distinguish one twin from another by means of astrology, using the fact that the order of births is known and therefore the differences that exist between the two charts.

Suzel Fuzeau-Braesch[7] has devised a simple technique for testing whether astrology could account for the differences observed between fraternal twins. She decides, on the basis of the two charts, the appropriate question for distinguishing between the twins. For example the question could be: 'Is X more energetic than Y?' This question would be appropriate if Mars were near one of the angles (Ascendant, Descendant, Midheaven or Nadir) and if for one of the twins Mars were closer to the angle than for the other. If no planet is near to an angle ($\pm$ 15°) then a possible change of sign by the ascendant may have occurred and this too would offer a means of distinguishing between the twins through an appropriate question. Finally, if there is no change of sign by the ascendant between the births, then the position of the ascendants within one sign can be considered. Given that one of them is nearer to an adjacent sign than the other, a question can be framed to make use of that fact. For example, if twins are born with ascendants at 16° and 22° of Gemini, the first could be expected to be 'more mobile, more expansive' and the second 'less expansive, more attached to mother' (corresponding to Cancer, the next sign).

Most of the forms containing the questions were completed by parents (most of the twins were under seventeen). A few were completed by one of the twins or by another member of the family. For the experiment 238 replies were received and because the test is a very simple one (either right or wrong), one could expect that about half of the replies would be correct and a half incorrect by chance. In fact 153, rather than 119, were correct. This is a very large deviation from expectation and the odds of it occurring by chance are more than 1000 to 1 against. There are a number of features of the experiment which make it unlike Gauquelin's work:

(1)   All of the planets including Mercury and the outer planets, Uranus, Neptune and Pluto, plus the Sun and Moon were used.

(2)   The zodiacal signs were used, either for a change of sign or else for the angular distance to an adjacent sign.

(3)   The excess of correct replies occurred both for natural births and for those that had been induced. Even for births by caesarian section the excess persisted.

(4)   There was no significant difference between the results obtained for monozygotic or dizygotic twins, neither (in the case of dizygotic twins) between those of same sex and those of different sex. (Monozygotic twins are always of the same sex.)

(5)   The actual departure from chance expectation is very large compared with the deviations which Gauquelin measured.

These major differences between research results make one wonder whether the results of the Fuzeau-Braesch work could have derived from effects other than astrology. For example, occasionally results of similar experiments have been shown to be strongly affected by 'self-attribution'. This can arise if subjects know what would be expected astrologically and write answers which conform.

Most people know what their sun-signs are, because the dates of the year applying to occupancy by the Sun of each of the signs are published in newspapers which carry features on 'You and your Stars'. People also know the kind of personality traits expected from a Piscean, a Taurean etc. Thus when asked a question which is clearly aimed at distinguishing a particular sun-sign trait it is easy for an individual to respond with a confirming answer, even though it may not be particularly applicable. This problem of self-attribution appeared in an experiment carried out by Mayo[8] in collaboration with White and Eysenck involving 2,000 respondents answering a questionnaire to deduce an extroversion/introversion score. The results indicated that those with the Sun in traditionally 'positive' signs: Aries, Gemini, Leo, Libra, Sagittarius and Aquarius appeared to be significantly more extrovert than those born with the Sun in 'negative' signs: Taurus, Cancer, Virgo, Scorpio, Capricorn and Pisces. However, it turned out that the subjects were mainly students of astrology who were well aware of the interpretations placed on the sun-signs. An ingenious statistical device demonstrated that self-attribution lay behind the results. The subjects were split into three groups:

1. Experienced students, well versed in all branches of astrology.
2. Those knowing only the signs of the zodiac.
3. Those knowing nothing of astrology.

The significant association was found to persist only for the second group. The plausible explanation for this finding is that those with no knowledge of astrology would not bias the outcome. Similarly, those experienced students, aware of many other factors in the chart, would not be unduly influenced by sun-signs. It would be unsound to call this explanation more than 'plausible' unless there were corroborative evidence. However, it should be mentioned that Pawlik and Buse have demonstrated the same tendency for people, knowing their sun-signs, to bias answers they give to personality assessment questionnaires.

Now, in the case of the Fuzeau-Braesch experiment, it seems very unlikely that there could be any self-attribution operating, or any bias introduced by a parent knowing the astrological differences between their twin children. In the first place, the experiment is not using sun-signs, and secondly, the main method of distinguishing between twins was the 'rocking sign' technique (which has been described above using the example of twins born with their ascendants at 16° and 22° of Gemini) and this technique was actually invented for the purpose of the experiment – and so could not be known to the subjects.

Clearly, this experiment has great interest for researchers. It opens up a new area for investigation. Up to now, fraternal twins have been something of an embarrassment to astrologers – because the question arises of why dizygotic twins are no more alike than pairs of ordinary siblings. There is no problem about monzygotic twins – they are very similar and astrology says they should be. But astrology also says that dizygotic twins ought to be similar (having been born at a similarly short interval from one another as monzygotic twins), and all the statistical work measuring their personality traits, their intelligence quotients, their propensity to suffer from disease – even their criminal tendencies – indicates that they are no more alike than pairs of siblings. This suggests that the only factor playing any measurable part is the genetic component. Monozygotic twins start with identical genetic inheritances and indeed they are very similar. The genetic inheritance of dizygotic twins is no more similar than that of any pairs of siblings. Occasionally astrologers will argue that there are important time differences between the births which 'explain' this away. But, in fact, the data[9] show that the average interval between the births of monozygotic and dizygotic twins is not significantly different.

Hence, this work by Fuzeau-Braesch is highly encouraging for traditionalists. Not only does it appear that distinguishing between twins astrologically is a possibility but also that the 'first cry' of the infant is the significant time (i.e. intervention with the birth time has no discernible effect, contrary to Gauquelin's findings). Finally, the use of the zodiacal signs is another fillip for traditional astrology. Researchers had come to despair of ever finding evidence to support belief in the signs.

The Problems of Research

The brief summary of recent research given above illuminates several of the pitfalls which face investigators. The chief problems that lie in wait are:

(1) *Selection of the Data*

This was noted in respect of the Vernon Clark type experiments described earlier. If there is any opportunity to select data which support the case then the findings are suspect. The fact that Clark had chosen the subjects who were to be 'matched' with their charts immediately raises the question of whether subjects had been selected because they 'fitted' their horoscopes.

The same problem was noted in judging reports about time twins which appear in the press. How many differences between the twins have been ignored in order to make 'a good story'? In other words, the adverse facts had been 'selected out'.

(2) *Self Attribution*

The snare of self-attribution was noted in discussion of the Mayo experiment described above. It is a problem that arises most acutely when investigations are made into sun-sign effects. However, occasionally it has been suggested as the reason for the apparent success of other, non sun-sign, researches. Some years ago an article appeared in the *Biologist*[10] arguing that a mother-to-be would be concerned that her child be born at an auspicious time, i.e. with a planet 'well-placed' in the diurnal circle, and that this could influence birth time or even the recording of the birth time. This was intended to be an explanation for the Gauquelin results on collections of professionals. It goes beyond self-attribution to the idea of direct influence on birth time in order to achieve astrological benefit. In fact, this attempt at refutation fails when it is appreciated that the Gauquelin auspicious planetary areas do not coincide with the traditional ones, so that even if the first requirements for the refutation to be successful were present (parental knowledge of the traditional planetary influence in relationship to the angles and knowledge of the current position of the planets in the sky) this would still not provide a means of amplifying the Gauquelin effect.

(3) *Attributing Significance Inappropriately*

It is a great temptation to attach significance to striking coincidences. The difficulty arises from the means used to judge whether a particular coincidence is indeed very unlikely or merely appears so. One piece of evidence offered to support the idea that time twins share similar characteristics is the fact that Albert Einstein and the Nobel prize-winning physicist Otto Hahn were both born on 14 March 1879. Let us suppose that every year, throughout the world, some five people are born who will later become outstanding physicists. The probability that none of these five will share a birthday is:

$$\frac{364}{365} \times \frac{363}{365} \times \frac{362}{365} \times \frac{361}{365} = 0.9729$$

Einstein and Hahn were born in 1879. A period of fifty years would take us up to 1929 and anyone born as late as 1929 would have made his or her mark as a physicist by now. So what is the probability that during any one of these years there would have been no pairs of famous physicists born on the same day of the same year? The answer is:

$$(0.9729)^{50} = 0.2532$$

Thus the probability that at least one of such pairs could have occurred is:

$$1 - 0.2532 = 0.7468$$

In other words the chance is about 3 to 1 in favour of finding at least one such pair. Far from its being remarkable, we could have expected this sort of thing to have happened again since 1879, entirely by chance.

The Need For Research On Time Twins

This brief list of some of the commonest pitfalls that beset the researcher indicates why systematic research into time twins is needed. It is quite easy to be deluded by accounts of time twins. The resemblances could have arisen by chance, or the accounts could have been subject to biased selection so that dissimilarities have been omitted. On the other hand, to succeed in showing that the time twin effect is real would be a mile-stone in the story of astrological research.

The first point is that the existence (if such can be demonstrated) of time twins is very powerful evidence of a time dependency operating. It is not necessary to invoke astrology. The time dependence could arise from any factor whose influence changes over time. For example, one could suppose that the characteristics of a person derive partly from the intensity of illumination by sunlight at the time of birth. In this case, it would follow that people born at the same time tended to share characteristics. It would be necessary to have demonstrated some additional planetary correlation for astrology to come into the picture.

The second point is that one does not have to get the astrology right for the time twin effect to work. We could be using the wrong zodiac (some astrologers prefer a sidereal zodiac to the most favoured tropical one) or we could have got the important locations of planets wrong (favouring angular rather than cadent houses as Gauquelin found) or we could be looking at the wrong planets (Gauquelin found nothing deriving from Sun, Mercury or the outer planets) or we could be ignoring influential heavenly bodies such as the fixed stars. Thus, time twin research is more fundamental than the other sorts of investigation that have been mounted. It actually suggests another powerful method for constructing astrology from scratch. If two time twins resemble one another then their characteristics can be compared with their horoscope to *derive* the connections (rather than accept them on trust from traditional beliefs) and thus build up, piece by piece, an empirical astrology.

The next chapter is concerned with the 'Mirror Images' project which preceded the time twins research and which was instrumental in initiating that research.

Chapter 3

Mirror Images

I am in conversation with a friend in the rear of a long, narrow antique shop. The door opens with the usual jingle of an old bell. We look, and lo, in walks my double. His build is mine – instantly I am uneasy, hostile. By what right has this stranger to duplicate me? By the time he has walked to where we are, he is clearly annoyed at finding me, his double, sitting there, duplicating his mannerisms, posture, voice. He forgets what he came in to tell my friend, begins struggling to cope with the shocking experience of meeting an astrological twin. We can literally feel each other's mind, feel each other marvelling at the likeness, and we both feel invaded, discovered.

Al H. Morrison *On Meeting Astrological Twins*[1]

At basic levels astrology can be a hobby, a parlour game, an amusement or diversion; in all, it can be great fun.

Beyond such levels, astrology becomes whatever one wants. For me it was the start of a personal journey, revealing personal strengths yet admitting to and facing personal weaknesses. Astrology opens doors; it makes one aware of alternative courses of action. If the individual attempts an honest review of personality, astrology allows him to act more responsibly, increasingly aware of the consequences of his actions.

Being an astrologer is more complicated! Having built an astrological consultancy practice on recommendation only, now I admit to wanting just one client – me. Faced with a client desperately in need of advice, who asks the astrologer to play God and to determine the outcome of their actions can be tiresome and demanding. At the end of the day, the clients must make their own choices *guided* by the astrology of the time. It is my experience that clients do this best when their life is not surrounded by pain and upset, yet ironically this is most usually the time when people seek guidance.

The mistake perhaps, and one fostered by the media, is that astrology is believed to be predetermined, our lives fated by some blueprint map over which we have no control. Anyone studying astrology to any real depth will appreciate that there exists a fine line between fate and free will and that life is a mixture of both. For example, it is a fact of life that at some time we will experience bereavement, the pain of losing someone close to us. It is obvious that even if we possessed total free will we would still experience this pain, but would anyone willingly choose to go through the experience of mourning? And yet, the bottom line is that in order to get over such losses we must fully experience them – whether immediately in a generally healthy way or at some delayed date as trauma.

Astrology offers guidance. It helps us come to terms with the necessity to experience that it is really OK to feel bewildered, frightened, angry, sorrowful, guilty and the miriad of emotions one can experience when losing someone close. Astrology gives us licence to grieve and reassures that, given time, we will move on with renewed promise and vigour for life. Astrology simply helps us understand our own tapestry of time and to develop our skills more fully and, I believe, more individually.[2]

Whatever readers may conclude – whether astrology be a parlour game and full of nonsense or that there exists something of greater value – I will bet that there isn't one who, sitting in their garden in the gentle breeze of a summer evening looking up at a full moon night sky, has not been touched by such reverence and beauty. And in this light it seems easy to suppose there really is some resonance between the heavenly bodies and the inhabitants of earth.

My interest in the study of astrology came about quite by chance. A friend 'did' my chart one Saturday afternoon and I was struck by the accuracy of his interpretation. It was a time in my life of crossroads and uncertainty as to direction in the areas of career and relationships; it was an appropriate time to seek guidance. Circumstances contrived to introduce me to the world of astrology, and to a greater quality of living. Astrologers among you would suggest the time had arrived for such guidance and that 'there it was, in my chart!'

Yet years later as I now sit facing blank pages to be covered in at least a vaguely legible manner by solid print, I am tempted to flights of fancy to persuade my reader that the same astounding coincidences which heralded my interest in astrology likewise marked my foray into the world of astrological twins!

No so. There is nothing remarkable about the project's origins.

In my thirst for knowledge I read anything relating to astrology. Out of work and taking time out from life, it seemed I had days in which to contemplate and study. It happened that one day I picked up a copy of the magazine *Prediction* which at the time carried a Personal Ads section, and in particular an 'Astro-Twins' column. Here were persons identified only by their birth-date and a desire to locate their time twin soul mate.

I have to admit that the idea did intrigue me. I was readily persuaded by the idea that somewhere 'out there' existed someone just like me. I pondered the idea of meeting another me and wasn't sure whether I would feel enthusiastic or rather disappointed if, after all, I discovered that I was not unique. Intrigue and curiosity led me further, and it was not long before my own advertisement adorned *Prediction*'s Classified Ad section – it read:

Scorpio lady born 12 Nov. 1958 seeks astro-twin for friendship
and life comparison. Reply Box E508. [or words to that effect]

I received one reply, from a woman whose daughter had been born twelve hours earlier than me. Her letter was friendly but gave little detail and I replied with brief autobiographical history. So began a lengthy correspondence between Sheila and myself. There were some basic similarities between her daughter Susan and myself. We had both worked in a winebar; had both had relationships with men called Brian; both our fathers were connected with the sea. New to the 'idea' of astrological twins any small and meaningless fact blindingly and understandably persuaded me that there would be some synchronicity in our lives.

Now I reflect upon such naivety.

What did strike a chord was that I had cause to talk to Sheila, the mother, on the telephone one evening and it turned out her birthday was a day later than that of my own mother. Sheila's personality and life patterns are very different from my dear mother but in tone, voice and expressions, if I had not known otherwise, I would have sworn that this was *my* mother talking to me which, to this day, has left a lasting impression.

It will come as no great surprise to astrologers reading this, that the lifestyle and personality between Susan, her daughter, and myself are very different. While we were born on the same day our time of birth

differs by twelve hours. I was born with the sign of Taurus on my Ascendant position, suggesting a personality of practicality, steadfastness and
commonsense. My astrological day twin born twelve hours earlier has
Scorpio on her Ascendant accentuating her Sun in Scorpio and suggesting
a far more intense and passionate nature. Furthermore, her moon – of
importance in determining the emotional nature of the persona – is also in
Scorpio, further highlighting Susan's strong Scorpio nature. I was born
later and the moon had of course travelled through Scorpio into the
following sign of Sagittarius, suggesting that my emotional nature would
be more spirited and changeable.

Despite these obvious factors I continued to be intrigued by the notion
of astrological twins and the idea of a twin soul-mate. I was eager to make
contact with someone born more closely to my time of birth.

As with everything in life synchronicity often contrives to provoke
circumstance and it was not long after that I noticed an advertisement,
again in *Prediction*, purporting to 'find your astrological twin, cost
£10.00'. I eagerly forwarded my money but to this day have never had a
reply. I often wonder how many others despatched £10.00?

It was my Scorpio fixity – or perhaps my Taurean desperate need to
acquire – that piqued me sufficiently for me to consider establishing a
service bureau to which persons could apply to trace their astrological
twin, and so the ideas of Mirror Images slowly began to take shape.

In astrology the moment an idea bears fruition and puts into practice
some new event, that moment in time becomes of essence, marking the
birth of the enterprise for which a horoscope can be erected and an interpretation given. On 18 January 1987 my partner Brian and I were travelling
back from Cambridge by train on a bitterly cold winter's afternoon and the
train was stationary just outside Bishop's Stortford. Why this image remains vivid is somewhat of a mystery but it was there, at approximately
four in the afternoon, that the decision to launch Mirror Images was made.

Initially the idea had been to simply establish a bureau service to trace
astrological twins. The notion that it could be combined with a research
study followed, though quite what prompted it is unknown.

But there it was, and the idea was simple.

Anyone could register and if we were successful in locating at least two
people who could be termed 'participating twins' they would be invited to
complete a simple questionnaire, the purpose of which was to 'fully
investigate the phenomenon of astrological twins'.

Now began the hard work. I had little funds and began by writing to
each of the local astrological groups throughout the UK inviting participa-

tion in the project. Anyone could write in and register. Little by little word got round and provoked interest from the media.

I also sought to advise the astrological fraternity of my intention and Charles Harvey, President of the Astrological Association, was kind enough to forward an article written by John Addey, an erudite astrologer, written in 1966.

John Addey,[3] a pioneer in astrological research and technique, had collected a selection of examples of astrological twins, some of which are mentioned in Chapter 1. It is of course easy to compile an impressive list of the 'coincidental' cases. I have a box of such examples from the media, all of which will 'fit' the notion that astrological time twins' lives do bear a certain resemblance. Addey made a complete inventory of four volumes of *Who Was Who* and compiled a list of coincident birthdays, publishing all those who had reached their ninetieth year. As Addey states: 'clearly one could expect nothing similar among them except their eminence and their age'. One of those detailed, reproduced below, shows how closely parallel two men's lives ran:

Case 1. Born 17 December 1856

Name:	Meyers, Rev Charles	Ashmall, Rev Francis
Status:	Not married	Married, no children
Assistant curate:	Wantage 81-85	Farnham 81-86
Vicar:	Lyme Regis 88-94	Southampton 86-89
Rector:	Salisbury 94-15	Bishopstoke Hickling 96-28
Rural Dean:	Wilton 14-19	S Bingham 06-28
Canon	Salisbury Cathedral	(Hon. Canon) Southwell 18-
Residentiary:	15-27	28
Died:	Aged 92 years 2 months	Aged 92 years 4 months

Addey's work was only a pilot study and its conclusions are, of course, quite unsubstantiated in terms of validated statistical and scientific analysis, yet it surprised me that no one has attempted to follow up his work, particularly as he concluded:

> . . . I hope the evidence mustered in this article may encourage someone, either inside or outside astrological circles, to follow up research on this subject of coincident births . . .

Addey's article did inspire me and though my methods could be criticised in the area of research I nevertheless began to amass articles and reported incidences of coincidences where two or more people shared the same birthdate.

People involved in the project would send me newspaper clippings and articles reporting on amazing coincidences in the lives of people with coincident birth dates. These tended to be isolated cases and, as will be discussed, more attributable to chance coincidence than any evident corresponding birth time. The article by Addey was the first serious attempt to investigate the common cry from the astrological fraternity that persons born within close time proximity will share personality characteristics.

If astrological belief is so – that the time of birth and the astrology of that time heralds certain patterns of behaviour and personality – then the only 'proof' (and I use this word very loosely) must come from an examination of persons born close together in time, who share nothing in common except their birth time.

Whatever conclusions this book may draw I urge interested researchers to examine the parameters of such a research idea.

(A similar project was set up in 1992 in the United States, called 'Time Twins'.[4] Time Twins are finding similar difficulties in the collection of data as Mirror Images but it will be interesting to compare results when they have some data to work on.)

The more I came into contact with respected astrologers and communicated the idea of the project, the more convinced I became that, in the area of astrological time twins, there remained a void and one that should be addressed by research astrologers as a cornerstone for examining the fundamental claims of astrology.

Such a statement is easily made but not as easily executed.

While I had abundant energy and determination to succeed, the logistics of Mirror Images were difficult in two key areas: namely, the collection of the birth date register and the research technique used to compare personality.

If I might address the collection of a birth data register first.

It became apparent early on in the project that matching one individual with another, while sounding simple enough, requires an enormous data collection. For example, if you take only people born in 1958 then a data base of at least 365 x 2 will be needed to match every person born in 1958 with someone else born within a 24-hour period. You will need a sufficiently higher multiple of 365 if you wish to match the time of birth closely, say to within 15 minutes. And you will need an enormously higher multiple given, say, a spanning age generation of twenty years. It became obvious early on that my data base needed to be gigantic in order that I might effectively 'match' a birth date. The probability of a match based on the Mirror Images data collection method is mentioned in Chapter 4. When the Astrological Research Project was launched with Peter Roberts' joint involvement this particular problem was in part resolved.

A secondary problem with regard to any large data collection which concerns people is that of their contact addresses. People registering in 1987, and thus very early in Mirror Images' history, may not have been 'twinned' until 1990 or even later, by which time they may have moved and hence might no longer be in contact or contactable. Or their interest in the subject may have died and thus subsequent questionnaires receive no response.

The second problem was the question of research technique – how to compare one individual with another. It is important to note here that while I remain a lay person in the area of research techniques I hope to convince readers of the necessity for constructive and controlled research if embarking on such a course.

Having established an albeit scant register with matches arrived at by sheer chance, the next step was to build a questionnaire. After great deliberation Brian and I devised our own questionnaire.

In astrology the horoscope is divided into twelve houses, with each house said to have an association with specific areas in life. For example, the second house, ruled by Taurus and planet Venus, is said to bear an association with one's values in life – financial and material assets, wealth, money, income, resources and whatever is held dear to that person. Our questionnaire was devised so as to relate specifically to each house; for example, in the context of the Second House we asked the following questions:

2a. If employed, what is your bracket of financial earnings?
 £ 5,000-10,000
 £10,000-15,000
 £15,000-20,000
 £20,000 +
 I am unemployed

2b. What personal skills do you use most, for example carpentry, photography etc.?

2c. Are you an avid collector of any specific objects?

It was our attempt to build a profile of the interests, direction and type of person. The finished questionnaire spanned some six pages, requested intensely personal information and lacked design. Anyone with any knowledge of research techniques will see just how crude an attempt this was for a valid research tool.

In the first instance it is probably impossible to build a statistically viable and valid research questionnaire designed to compare life experiences. What stands out in one person's mind as an important event may be quite inconsequential to another. Life itself carries such a huge array of experiences that it is impossible to take into account every conceivable event and rate these according to importance and impact. Life experiences and 'impact' are affected by upbringing, race, culture and circumstance and might be quite different for a number of people, even if their birthdays *are* the same.

Throughout the research project I have been at pains to explain this point and *still* the media persist in wanting to explore the concept that astrological twins will experience coincident and similar events in their lives!

As may be expected, the response rate to this initial crude questionnaire was negligible and it was soon abandoned. I sought the advice of the more experienced astrologers involved in long term research including Françoise Gauquelin, Charles Harvey, Geoffrey Dean and Lois Rodden and many others. All were so tremendously helpful and I am indebted to their continued support of the project.

Charles Harvey kindly introduced Brian and me to Professor Hans Eysenck of the University of London who explained the various pitfalls in astrological research and the need for defined and validated questionnaires, not to mention necessity for replication of a study, statistical methodology and control groups.

Questionnaires need careful and structured construction. The questions themselves need to be selected and tested on representative samples of population to demonstrate that they actually measure what is intended to be measured.

Anyone can establish a research study, much as Brian and I had done, but unless you go about it in the right way the results may lead to meaningless muddle. As a tool our questionnaire was invalid. It was too lengthy, too personal and left too much room for indirect and oblique answers. Over a year's efforts had amounted to nothing.

It is also worth noting that *any* research which relates directly to astrological factors will require accurate birth data, namely, time, date and place of birth. In England the fact that the time of birth is not recorded on the birth certificates (except in the case of multiple births) severely hampers and restricts valid research parameters. It is not sufficient to rely on parental memory and approximate birth times.

Given that there is a suggestion that modern day medical interference in the birth process, i.e. by caesarean or drug inducement, negates the natural astrological patterns and resonance, a further distortion can be expected in any research project.

I am sure that many other faults can be found in the parameters of the Mirror Images project but its initial (and remaining) goal was to 'set the ball rolling' in the area of establishing defined research into time twins.

After deliberation, and following further advice from Geoffrey Dean, we decided to use the standard Eysenck Personality Questionnaire.

Mirror Images' main thrust changed from looking at life circumstances and events and their similarity *or* dissimilarity to personality assessment, making comparisons based upon certain model behaviour.

There seems to survive throughout the ages the four cornerstone personality 'types' rooted in ancient discipline, myth and legend.

Astrology	Fire	Earth	Air	Water
Alchemy	Choleric	Melancholic	Sanguine	Phlegmatic
Jung	Feeling	Sensation	Thinking	Intuitive

The Eysenck Personality Questionnaire looks similarly at four personality 'types' described as Extroverted (E), Psychoticism (P), Neurotic (N) and tendency toward self deception (L). Questionnaires are designed to score against a scale measuring the E, P, N, L personality. The fundamentals of the Eysenck Personality Questionnaire is well documented in the literature but briefly, it may be seen that the personality is measured according to these brief statements:

E: outgoing, gregarious
P: disregard for others, ruthless
N: moody, prone to self doubt
L: self deception, illusory self valuation, conceit

In such questionnaires, determining if a person tends toward extroversion can be made by asking such questions (taken from the Eysenck Questionnaire) as:

Are you rather lively?

Can you usually let yourself go and enjoy yourself at a lively party?
Do you like plenty of bustle and excitement around you?
Do other people think of you as being very lively?

I am aware that the Eysenck Personality Questionnaire has its critics but its strength lies in the extensive use it has had and its validation in terms of repeatability and relationships with sex, age and profession.

Mirror Images moved on with a more acceptable Questionnaire format but still facing the difficult problem of the collection of data. Progress was slow and I began to wonder if there was any reason to continue with the project.

In 1989, I was introduced to Peter Roberts and at last it seemed I was able to put the project on a firmer footing. The Astrological Research Project (ARP) was launched as an adjunct to Mirror Images using the same EPQ questionnaire and similar outline but was confined to seeking persons born on *specific* dates rather than a random collection of time twins. The results of this and the pilot study of Mirror Images are discussed in detail in Chapter 4.

Whatever the parameters required by the hard scientific world in requirement of statistical and solid 'evidence' or 'proof' there remains a need to 'believe' in the principle of astrological twins – that two people, sharing the same birth date and close time of birth will experience extraordinary coincidental experiences.

And so perhaps it is time to look at several of these 'amazing' and 'astounding' coincidences. The Mirror Images register is not necessarily a good source for coincidences simply because, having based its efforts around personality assessment, the project is not designed to single out the similarities in experiences. Nevertheless, given the amount of material that has been forwarded to me from interested people, certain generalities are apparent.

On record we have several cases of pairs of twins who have written in to say they share the same Christian, middle or surname. Most striking of these was from a young girl who wrote to say, 'My friend is born on the same day, same month, same year, same time and same place as me. She also has the same name and the same middle name as me. Her mother and father share the same birthdates as my mother and father and also the same names.'

Given that names are often 'popular' – for example, when Kylie and Jason hit the pop scene a number of baby Kylies and Jasons were christened – then it is not so astounding to find a coincident name. To have both parents sharing the same birthday and name is possibly more astonishing.

Shared or coincident medical history can be striking. In the case of one of my own time twins, born eight hours later than myself, we shared a history of asthma and psoriasis. Given the fact that psoriasis is the most common skin disease and asthma a growing complaint, such coincidence seems not so revealing. However, I was surprised to find that both he and I were admitted to hospital within a week of one another for 'investigative' surgery and both left hospital none the wiser and with nothing medically wrong.

One of the questions the Mirror Images questionnaire asks is:

> 'What specific medical complaints or major illnesses, if any, do you or have you suffered from?'

A pair of twins separated in time by only 20 minutes and both born in London answered with 'pneumonia' which is a fairly unusual medical complaint for the under-50s. In another case, separated by some three hours, both answered that they had had tumours successfully removed but not without long-term distress.

It is my growing conviction that the medical history of astrological twins is likely to be the most revealing area giving 'proof' and 'hard evidence' for astrology. Whether any of the medical establishments would allow access for such a research project remains highly doubtful. Interestingly, in John Addey's article referred to earlier, Addey mentions a collection of birth dates of sufferers from poliomyelitis with a given time of birth and age at which polio was contracted. The findings suggested that the percentage contracting polio at the same age falls steadily as the interval between the births grows.

There then exist many cases of '. . . my astrological twin and I married on the same day.' Again, with a little insight such factors are hardly likely to be striking factual proof that time twins share fate and experience. Statistics will reveal that the average age of marriage is between 20 and 30, the most popular months of the year to get married in are the summer months, and the most popular day of the week for a wedding is Saturday. It is unlikely to be anything other than chance coincidence.

Where there are lists of similarities one may well expect there to be some factor at work. In the case of Pauline and Irene the list does read as quite impressive:

	Pauline	Irene
Birthdate	7 September 1947	ditto
	Newcastle Maternity	ditto
	Hospital 'within six hours	
	of one another'	
Marriage Date	6 September 1969	ditto
Marriage Time	13.30	13.09
Husband's Name	Dennis William	William
Husband's Birthdate	11 January 1947	18 January 1948
Husband's School	'same as one another'	
Address	'both Pauline and Irene lived around the corner from one another in end-semis'	
Children	'attended the same playgroup, nursery and school'	
Employment	'ledger clerk in same office and both started as punch machine operators'	
Mother's birthday	9 July	5 July
Mother's status	divorced	ditto
Mother's sisters	died early at age 21	ditto at age 18
Medical history	TB at age 4	Pneumonia in first weeks of life
	neck problems	ditto
Physical likeness	'both slim, weight conscious, dark haired'	

A report in the *Chatham News* in November 1988 describes the thread of coincidences running through the lives of neighbours Angela and Barbara, both born on the same day. Twelve years ago they lived next door to one another and discovered their youngest children shared the same birthday and were both born by caesarean section. Both work as school dinner ladies, have the same shoe size and frequently return home from shopping trips having bought the same products. When Angela broke her left wrist, Barbara crushed her left elbow.

More tragically, the *Express News*, Texas, of May 1989[5] reports the case of Jacqueline Johns Wiatrek and Billy Wayne Mutz who were born within hours of one another in the same hospital. At the age of twenty-one both died in unrelated traffic accidents on the same evening.

And so the list of coincidences goes on. Perhaps the most grim and peculiar case we have is that of a pair of time twins born in South Africa.

Kathryn and Corrin, known to one another throughout their youth, naturally grew apart as the years passed, particularly from the time Kathryn came to live in England. Kathryn returned to South Africa for a three-week holiday, not realising that Corrin was at the time in England on holiday. While in South Africa, Kathryn had a vivid dream that her leg was to be amputated, a dream that disturbed her greatly despite her nursing career. It turned out that the night Kathryn had this gruelling dream, Corrin was in England undergoing amputation surgery having contracted a rare form of meningitis.

An exhaustive search of the media would no doubt reveal many time twin cases of astounding, astonishing and unexpected coincidence. But if I were to meet my own twin, or just to select a person at random from the street, I am sure that if I delved long and hard enough I would collect a similar list of 'astounding' similarities. Where the newspapers report such incidences it seems far more attributable to chance than to any shared astrological birth detail.

Are we correct to seek such duality of existence? We cannot really expect to find the lives of astrological twins falling into such repetitive, robotic dual patterns since astrology teaches that we do have free will, that circumstance and the people around us, our culture, race and background all affect our own astrological 'identity'. In Chapter 1 there is an historical account of the chimney sweep and the king. The king, born into a life of royalty and patronage, we assume is likely to have greater opportunity to direct the course of his life than the poor chimney sweep who struggles to make ends meet.

It is interesting that in the myth of Castor and Pollux, the Heavenly Twins, there exists a *fundamental* difference. Castor was mortal and slain during battle, whereas Pollux was immortal and grieved the loss of his brother. Zeus, displaying compassion for the twins, allowed the brothers to enjoy alternately the boon of life on Earth and life in Heaven. The twins reflect a cyclical experience of opposites. The sign of Gemini is closely associated to the idea of sibling twins yet no other sign is quite as contrary as Gemini, given to being two things at any one time. Myth suggests that twins are unlikely to experience life in the same way: rather by necessity they develop different paths while remaining strongly attached to one another. They may have been born from the same egg but their free will allows them to exercise *choice* in how they develop their skills.

Finally – if it is so, that time twins share some coincidental thread of experience coupled with many similar personality characteristics, I am left with a degree of uncertainty; confronting someone as much like me as even a reversed reflection in the mirror is not without its terror! Providing certain fundamental differences exist I can remain confident that I am indeed, if nothing else, 'unique'.

Chapter 4

The Time Twins Project

The Pilot Experiment

Astrological research is demanding. Michel Gauquelin spent a large proportion of his life in the collection and analysis of his cases. Even when collections of birth data for specific categories of subject exist already (for example, the listing of all British army officers in this century) the astrological researcher is faced with many hours of analysis. As with research in other fields, it is wise to make the initial investigation on a small scale – a pilot experiment. There is no point in wasting effort by embarking on a full scale trial only to find that there is no evidence supporting the initial hypothesis. Gauquelin would never have worked through the tens of thousands of cases in his collections if he had not observed the striking distribution of Saturn in his initial experiment on the birth charts of scientists and physicians.

It would not have been a sensible enterprise to seek out clusters of time twins unless a pilot experiment showed that there was reason to expect interesting results from the larger trial. Accordingly, the Mirror Images register was scanned for cases of pairs of people born on the same day and for whom there had been completed psychological questionnaires. (In the earlier period of Mirror Images, a more elaborate general questionnaire had been employed, but this was non-standard and could not be used for comparison purposes. Thus, only subjects from the later period could be included in this pilot.)

It might be thought that all the work on time twins could have been done from the Mirror Images register but a little arithmetic shows that a random distribution of birth dates over some decades is a poor source of time twins.

When a general request is made for people to join the register, those replying cover a whole range of ages. Suppose that we have 1,000 cases spread over three decades. The spread is unlikely to be uniform, but for simplicity assume that it is.

The probability of one birth on a particular day is 1000/10958 = .09126 (10958 days because there are assumed to be 8 leap years in 30 years.)

Using the Poisson[1] distribution we find that the expected distribution of days with 0 births, 1 birth, 2 births, etc. is:

Number of births	Number of days when that number of births occurs	Number of births
0	1002	0
1	913	913
2	42	84
3	1	3
4+	negligible	0
	10958	1000

From the third row of the table, we can see that there are about 42 days when it could be expected that there would be two of our subjects sharing birthdays (or rather sharing the same day of birth). A little further calculation shows that only about 3 of these 42 days would contain pairs who were born less than an hour apart and if we accept a separation up to 6 hours between their birth times there would still be only about 18 of the 42 days when this could be expected to happen.

This calculation, incidentally, shows that advertisements which claim that 'Your time twin can be found' (from a general register) are being somewhat economical with the truth. Most registers will not be measured in the thousands and therefore the chance of there being someone on the register with the same birth date as you is down at the 1 in 10 level and if you are looking for a time twin born within an hour or two your chance is nearer 1 in 100.

Nevertheless, for the purposes of carrying out a pilot experiment, even the relatively small number of cases contained in a register is worth using. If there is an appreciable effect, it will show up even with a small sample, though of course, to demonstrate a pattern with statistical significance, a much more substantial sample is required.

From the Mirror Images register, there were 14 pairs of subjects for whom we had completed questionnaires and with each pair having a birth time separation of less than 8 hours. From the psychological questionnaire, each member of a pair has an E score, an N score, a P score and an L score. Thus the difference of E scores between each member of a pair could be plotted against the separation in birth time. If there is any tendency for psychological profiles to be similar then a trend would be discernible in the plot of the points. In fact, a distinct trend appeared for each of the plots of N, P and L, though there was no trend apparent from the E plot.

A sample of 14 is very small from which to draw any conclusions. However, three out of four of the trends were in the 'right' direction, so there was encouragement to delve further. In order to make more use of the data, a composite measure was devised to determine an overall psychological separation between two subjects. Clearly, it is possible for two subjects to have closely similar E scores but to have N scores which are quite different (and similarly for E and P, P and N etc.). What is needed is

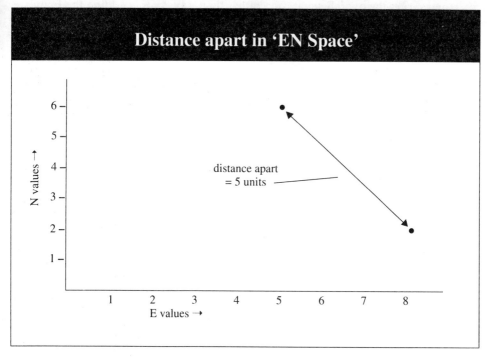

Fig. 4.1

a measure which combines the separations in such a way that each factor contributes to the overall separation.

Suppose that, for two subjects, the E values were 5 and 8 and the N values were respectively 6 and 2, we could think of these pairs of values set out in graphical form with an E axis and an N axis. In Figure 4.1 this has been done and the direct distance from one point to the other across the graph is 5 units. (Apart from direct measurement, the value of 5 corresponds to the hypoteneuse of the right angled triangle with sides of 3 and 4, because 8-5 = 3 and 6-2 =4. Furthermore, in Pythagorean triangles 5x5 = 3x3 + 4x4).

The idea of measuring the distance across EN space corresponds well to the underlying concept of distinct psychological factors. The factors have been chosen to be, as far as possible, independent. In technical language, they are supposed to be 'orthogonal' (which is another way of saying: 'at right angles to one another' in the same way as our axes are at right angles to one another). Thus, there is a good case for using this method of measuring the overall separation rather than, say, simply adding the E and N separations together to make 7.

The same technique can be used to measure the overall separation if three rather than two factors are taken into account. Instead of a plane with an E axis and an N axis, we would have a space with three axes of E, N and P. The overall separation distance would be across this three dimensional space. Suppose that the separation of the E values was 2 units and likewise 2 units for the N values and 2 units for the P values, then the overall separation would be $\sqrt{(2x2)+(2x2)+(2x2)} = \sqrt{12} = 3.46$.

With this method of determining overall separation, we can ask the question: 'Is the overall separation in NPL space correlated with the separation of birth times?' This is a different question from asking whether the N, P and L separations are each correlated with the birth time separation because, as was noted earlier, there is no *a priori* reason why a small separation in N values for a pair should be accompanied by a small separation in P values or a small separation in L values.

The separations in NPL space were calculated for the sample and a plot made of these values against the birth time separations. The plot is shown in Figure 4.2. It can be seen that there is a distinct trend present. In statistical terms there is a correlation coefficient of .65 and this result would occur by chance only about 1 in 100 times. However, it cannot be regarded as significant because there has been selection. The E separation values had been excluded because there seemed to be no trend present for the E factor. If it is permissible to exclude inconvenient results then one is

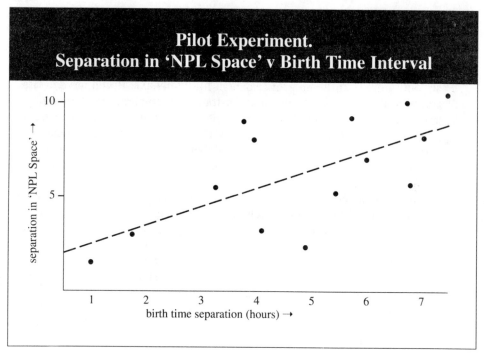

Fig. 4.2

very likely to see something remarkable! However, this is a very small sample and the reason for using it was to see if anything of interest emerged. The results are indeed encouraging and furthermore it is possible to formulate a hypothesis to be tested on quite new data. The hypothesis is that the overall separation in EPNL space of pairs of time twins will be correlated with their birth time separation. Note that this hypothesis contains all four factors rather than just N, P and L. There is no *a priori* justification for excluding any of the factors and hence all four have been included in the stated hypothesis.

It is important that a hypothesis be stated in advance of a trial, because if one is allowed to search for any sort of 'remarkableness' in the results of a trial, it is quite likely that something will be found. Every new possibility of remarkableness which is introduced lowers the significance of finding any one of them present. As a trivial example of this point, I recall at one time having colleagues who lived in houses with street numbers which were all the squares of integers (1, 9, 64 and 169). How astonishing, I thought, until it occurred to me that a rich variety of other sets of numbers would also have struck me as astonishing, e.g. all four having the same number such as 32, 32, 32, 32; the numbers being in order such as 53, 54, 55,56; all four being multiples of 10 such as 20, 10, 40, 100; or all four being prime such as 11, 23, 41, 53. If you were to list all the possible ways in which a set of four numbers could be 'apparently unusual' the chance of finding any one of these cases would be high (perhaps better than evens!). However, if you were to state in advance a particular hypothesis about the four numbers – such as all of them being the squares of numbers – then the chance of its actually occurring could be calculated accurately. As a matter of interest, if only numbers less than 100 are considered and there is a uniform chance of any one of them occurring, then obtaining 4 which are perfect squares would happen 1 in 10,000 times on average.

Choosing Dates

The pilot experiment showed that collecting data on time twins was likely to be rewarding. However, arithmetic on the register suggested that this would be a very slow method of finding time twins. It was decided to aim at specific days and to advertise for people who were born on one of those days. There were several considerations to be borne in mind. First, there should be a random element in the choice of dates to avoid the accusation that some 'special' date had been chosen (which, for example, had particular astrological significance). Secondly, it would be useful to spread the dates over some decades. Although one would prefer subjects who had already lived through many years of experiences (in order to be able to compare their experiences), there is likely to be a better response rate from younger subjects. Additionally, the 'time twin effect' may be evinced more strongly at some times than at others. Gauquelin had remarked on many occasions that the modern tendency to interfere with the natural moment of birth was a most undesirable development from the point of view of the astrological researcher. Those born earlier in the century were less likely to have births which had been induced or who to have been born by caesarian section. Thirdly, it would be necessary to strike a balance between naming a long list of days (in order to have a high response rate) and keeping the list short (in order that people would not be put off by the task of scanning the list to see if they or their friends were born on one of the chosen days).

It was decided to have six days at roughly seven year intervals, thereby covering about 35 years, and to start with the youngest subjects in their twenties. In order to arouse greater interest in the selected days, and also further to avoid any suggestion of particular choice of day, the days were to be the birth dates of well known people. It is known that people who share a birthday with someone prominent are often keenly aware of the fact and even nurse a certain pride in it. For example, they will sometimes contrive, in the course of conversation, to allude to the fact that they share a birthday with someone famous.

With the requirements described above, the protocol for choosing could be designed.

Six periods of time were set:

1 January 1928 - 31 December 1934
1 January 1935 - 31 December 1941
1 January 1942 - 31 December 1948
1 January 1949 - 31 December 1955
1 January 1956 - 31 December 1962
1 January 1963 - 31 December 1969

For each of these periods the names of well known people were selected: politicians, members of the royal family, tycoons, actors, writers, TV performers, singers, inventors. Despite the fact that there tend to be more prominent men than women, the selection was deliberately biased to obtain an equal number of men and women. Each person's name was written on a card and the cards for one period put into a hat. Dr Sarah Bruml (who is independent of the experiment and indeed sceptical of it) agreed to check that the cards in the hat were all different and then, having mixed them up, to choose one at random. By this means, the following six names (one for each of the time periods) were selected:

Dame Judi Dench	9 December 1934
Jilly Cooper	21 February 1937
Prince Charles	14 November 1948
Richard Branson	18 July 1950
Lenny Henry	29 August 1958
Lady Sarah Armstrong Jones	1 May 1964

Finding The Subjects

Having a list of birth dates, our next problem was to discover subjects who shared those birth dates. Furthermore, they had to be people who were willing to co-operate in the experiment, which meant that they had to 'volunteer'. It would have been useful to have run a national advertising campaign, explaining the purpose of the project and inviting volunteers who had the chosen birth dates. However, those who have been involved in such enterprises will know that a big advertising campaign is a prodigiously expensive undertaking, so we had to substitute ingenuity.

The device which brought in most replies was a slot on a BBC radio programme in which the interviewer (John Dunn) asked questions about the project and called for listeners to tell anyone who was born on one of our chosen dates to write (Freepost) to the Box number we had set up for the purpose. This was helped by the *Radio Times* agreeing to publish a letter which recalled the radio programme and repeated the six dates.

It was arranged for a letter to appear in the *Guardian* 'Notes and Queries' page which asked the question: 'Are there scientists trying to prove that astrology is true?' Among the replies was a reference to the time twins project. From that piece of publicity came an article in the *Times Higher Educational Supplement* and later, a two page spread in the *Daily Mail*.[2] Articles appeared in a number of journals (though these tended to have only modest circulation figures). We thought that at some point there might be enough publicity for some word-of-mouth transmission to have started and the 'snowball effect' to take over, but judging by questions asked of acquaintances at random, this never happened. There is such a stream of information from the media nowadays that each item competes with a host of others for attention, and unless there is some element really to catch the imagination, the day's news simply flows into the dustbin of the past leaving little trace.

There are about 2,000 people born every day in the UK. Not all of them will still be resident in this country (or even surviving!) How many will have heard of the project, via these various schemes to advertise it? In my more pessimistic moods, I estimated no more than 10% of the potential subjects. Then comes the hurdle for the potential subject of actually making contact with the project, by writing to the Box number. Only a small proportion of people are interested enough in something to write a letter about it. After all, it is only a matter of interest – we were not offering a prize or indeed, at this stage, anything which could be called an inducement. I estimated that of those potential subjects who had heard of the project only 10% would actually take the trouble to respond. Overall then, we might expect something like 1% of 2,000 or about 20 subjects for each of the six days. In the event, this estimate was not so very far out.

In the reply to each of those who wrote, we sent them:

• A description of the project and what we were trying to achieve
• A copy of the Eysenck Personality Questionnaire to complete
• A sheet on which we asked for personal details such as their time of birth
• A bookmark with the emblem of the project as a token 'thank you' gift

Not every reply to our package was helpful. Some people confused the dates, or thought we wanted anyone born on the birthday of a 'royal'. Occasionally the Eysenck Personality Questionnaire was thought to be intrusive (though by most standards the questions are harmless enough).

Analysis

As the completed questionnaires were returned they had to be marked to find their E, N, P and L scores. When nearly 100 completed questionnaires had been returned and marked, a preliminary analysis was carried out. Unlike the pilot experiment, where there were 14 pairs of time twins scattered over the days and the years, this time we had clusters of people, each of whom is surrounded by many possible time twins. We wanted to take into account all the possibilities for psychological resemblances. If you imagine a day of 24 hours with one person born at each hour, i.e. one at 1 a.m., another at 2 a.m., all the way through to 12 midnight, then you can appreciate that there are 23 pairs at one hour birth separation times:

> one at 1 a.m. and one at 2 a.m.
> one at 2 a.m. and one at 3 a.m.
> one at 3 a.m. and one at 4 a.m.
>
> .   .
> .   .
>
> one at 11p.m. and one at 12 midnight

Additionally there will be 22 pairs, each with 2 hours' birth separation time:

> one at 1 a.m. and one at 3 a.m.
> one at 2 a.m. and one at 4 a.m.
> one at 3 a.m. and one at 5 a.m.
>
> .   .
> .   .
>
> one at 10p.m. and one at 12 midnight

And to complete the total there will be:

> 21 pairs with 3 hours birth separation time
> 20 pairs with 4 hours birth separation time
> . . . .
> 1 pair with 23 hours birth separation time

In all, for this one day with 24 births there will be 1+2+3. . .+23 pairs of time twins or a total of 276 pairs. There are different possible methods of analysis. We could take the average separation in EPNL space of all the pairs with 1 hour separation, then the average for all the pairs with 2 hours separation and so on. Alternatively, we could see what the proportion of 'close resemblers' is at 1 hour separation, 2 hours etc. Either method can be subject to statistical tests which will establish the significance of the results. The method to be used will depend on which of two possibilities is the most likely:

1. All those who are born at a particular time share in the 'qualities of that moment of time' and will therefore tend towards a higher resemblance to one another than any of them will towards someone born at a different time.

2. Among those born at a particular time will be a few whose innate characteristics correspond closely to the 'planetary indicators' at that time and place.

Although, at first sight, these two statements appear similar, the observable effects corresponding to each will be quite different. If the first were true then the 'time twins effect' should be quite commonplace and we would all take it for granted that if two people were born close together in time they would resemble one another much more than either would to someone else of similar age but born at a different time. Now, even the most enthusiastic supporter of astrology has to admit that the 'time twins effect' is not commonplace. Geoffrey Dean[3] points out that in the last hundred years the Western countries should have produced more than ten million people born within one minute of each other and less than fifteen miles apart. If each of these people really did show strong resemblances to his or her time twin, then we would all know about it.

The alternative possibility, number two above, suggests that some people do 'reflect' the planetary pattern at their births. If this is so then there would be occasional occurrences of time twins (two people, born close together and both of whom are 'reflecting' the planetary pattern) with striking resemblances to one another. Now, this is indeed what seems to happen. The reason that newspapers report extraordinary cases of time twin likenesses is that they are rather uncommon. One of the questions that the time twins project might be expected to answer is: 'How frequently do time twins show strong similarities?'

Given that the method of analysis to be used appears to be indicated as 'finding the proportion of strong resemblers', there is merit in using both approaches. If the first method, using the average psychological separation of all the one-hour-apart twins and the average separation of the two-hour-apart twins etc. yields a significant result we would have to conclude that indeed the time twin effect is pervasive but needs a more subtle test to demonstrate it than simple observation. Alternatively, if only the second method produces a significant result, then the thesis that only some people 'reflect' the planetary pattern receives support.

Results Of The Analysis

The preliminary analysis with 95 subjects indicated that there was no support for the first hypothesis. Taking the average separation in EPNL space between time twins born up to 1 hour apart, then between 1 and 2 hours apart, etc., the results did not show that there was any strong tendency for the average psychological separation between time twins to be lower when they were born close together than when they were born further apart. The table below lists the values for average EPNL space distance apart at particular birth time separations.

Birth time interval	Average separation in 'EPNL space'
0 - 1 hour	8.32
1 - 2 hours	7.82
2 - 3 hours	8.04
3 - 4 hours	8.35

However, the second hypothesis indicated that the proportion of 'high resemblers' was greater for those time twins born close together than for the others. Figure 4.3 shows the way in which the proportion falls off as the birth time separation increases (for the whole sample received).

More replies were received but the rate was declining. We 'closed the books' when roughly a further 50% of completed questionnaires had been

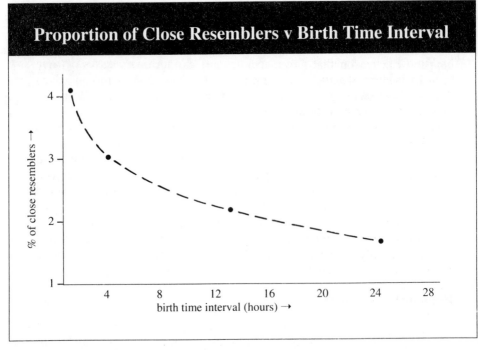

Fig. 4.3

received. This raised the total number of potential time twins from 748 on the first analysis with 95 subjects to 1,400 with 128 subjects. The additional subjects provided further confirmation of the finding already indicated by the first analysis. In order to be confident that the result was very unlikely to arise by chance, a detailed statistical check was carried out (see Appendix 5). This showed that the result could have arisen by chance about once in 300 such trials. To be really confident, one would like the significance level to be 1 in 1,000 and for the whole trial to be replicated, but given the problem of securing large samples, this is an encouraging outcome.

Interpretation

The subjects are not a random collection of individuals. If one asks for volunteers, then immediately there is a bias introduced, because the sort of people who volunteer are special – they have certain characteristics which are emphasised compared with the population at large. One indication of this is the distribution of E values among the subjects. There are more extroverts (people with high E values) in our sample than one would find in the general public. This is known because the Eysenck personality test has been used on a great variety of subjects and average scores are well established.

In itself, the slight emphasis on high E value subjects is not a big drawback – it could not account for the time twin effect which has been found. However, there is a further possibility which ought to be considered – that the sample is self-selecting for 'star born' subjects. Of the two hypotheses stated earlier, it has been found that the second received support. This was the one which postulated that a small proportion of people are 'star born' and reflect the planetary pattern at birth, i.e. whose personality characteristics correspond to their birth charts.

If there is any tendency for the 'star born' to volunteer in larger numbers than the rest of the population then our experiment will find a larger proportion of high resemblers than would be found in a random sample. It seems quite plausible that the 'star born' are drawn towards ideas associated with astrology. They would not necessarily be 'believers'. (A lot of intelligent people are badly put off by newspaper astrology.) However, they would lean towards a view of the world that could accommodate more subtle effects than are accepted in the standard scientific model – the idea of the planets being in some way involved with human life would not be alien to them.

If the ideas described above are sound then the proportion of high resemblers found in the time twins project is an upper limit. We can say that not more than 10% of time twins born within 3 hours of one another show any psychological resemblances closer than one could expect from two randomly chosen individuals (in Appendix 5 it is shown that the tendency for more close resemblers to occur persists beyond <3 in EPNL space – out to <5). The true proportion may be as low as 1%. There is some indication from Michel Gauquelin's[4] work on heredity that the proportion of 'star born' is quite low. He discovered a tendency for parents and their children to share the same prominent planets at birth, for example, if a mother had Jupiter rising then one or more of her children was more likely than chance to have Jupiter either rising or culminating – and similarly for the father and for the other planets. However, the effect is not a strong one. It was shown to be statistically significant because Michel used samples of tens of thousands. (In a later attempt at replication by associates of Gauquelin, no effect was found – this has never been satisfactorily explained). If only those cases where Michel found the parent/child planetary association are 'star born', this would suggest the proportion is about 3%.

There is a further item of evidence to suggest that the time twins project has found an upper limit rather than the true proportion. Checking for Gauquelin zone effects in the time twin subjects, the analysis (described in the next section) showed quite strong confirmation of the Gauquelin zones, but a similar experiment on several hundred randomly chosen subjects, carried out by a psychologist researcher, Beverley Steffert[5], found only a weak Gauquelin zone effect. This indicates that the time twin subjects are 'special' compared with a randomly chosen group.

Astrological Effects

It is of great interest to discover that there is a 'time twin effect', but one would also like to know if the origin of such resemblance derives from planetary influence – or simply, if there is any correspondence between the planetary pattern at birth and the personality characteristics of the subjects.

The most successful astrological research, as described in Chapter 2, has been that of Michel Gauquelin.[6] He showed firstly, that top professionals tended to be born with appropriate planets prominent in their birth charts, and secondly, that these same subjects tended to have personality characteristics (as revealed by their biographers) which conformed to the attributes associated with their prominent planets.

From the time twins project we have a group of subjects who have completed a standard psychological questionnaire and for whom we have, therefore, some information about their personality traits. The logical development of the research project would be to check whether the time twins subjects display any correspondence between their personality traits and their prominent planets. In order to use a high proportion of the subjects, we could test whether all those above average on any of the scales (the E, N, P, L scales) show any more tendency to have particular planets prominent than those below average. This check was carried out and demonstrated that there were no significant differences between the two groups on each of the scales. However, recalling that the 'average score' approach, described earlier and used for analysing the separations in EPNL space, was unfruitful, a different method was devised.

There is a theme running through successful astrological research. It can be summed up in the idea of 'seeking the exceptional'. Gauquelin's

triumph in demonstrating the astrological associations of his top professionals required the collection of groups comprising quite exceptional
athletes, scientists, generals, etc. The time twins project shows up an
interesting correlation between birth time interval and separation in 'psychological space' when the samples chosen are exceptional – because they
are 'close resemblers'. In the same way, we might expect any planetary
effects present in the time twins collection to emerge if we select for the
exceptional.

One way of selecting for the exceptional is to seek out the top scorers
on each of the scales (E, N, P, L). Clearly with only a modest sample, it is
not practical to choose, say, the top 1%. However, there will be some
cases to examine if the top 10% are extracted. Furthermore, if the (different) top 10% is used from each of the scales, and finally contrasted with
the lowest 10% as a control, then a large enough group will have been
assembled.

Gauquelin[7] found that the only planets to yield significant results when
he was looking for planetary associations with profession were Mars,
Jupiter, Saturn and the Moon (plus a later addition of Venus when he used
personality traits). Confining the search to the four 'Gauquelin planets',
we will have 16 possible planetary correlations (4 psychological traits,
each checked against 4 planets). It is convenient to use the Gauquelin
circle diagram (illustrated in Appendix 4) for demonstrating any potential
pattern.

Gauquelin Patterns

In order to pick out a possible Gauquelin pattern, the numbers of high E
scorers who have Jupiter in the 1st sector, the 2nd sector, etc. are to be set
out radially in the circle. However, there is a pitfall to be avoided. There is
likely anyway to be a variation in the total numbers of subjects with Jupiter
in the 1st sector, 2nd sector etc. The way to avoid this pitfall is to take the
proportion of high E scorers with Jupiter in the 1st sector out of the total
number of subjects with Jupiter in the 1st sector. By this means any
substantial underlying variation in the Jupiter numbers round the circle is
taken into account and the pattern which emerges derives solely from the
propensity of high E scorers to have Jupiter occupying particular sectors.

In Appendix 5 the pattern of Jupiter sector occupancies for high E
scorers has been calculated as a proportion of sector occupancies for all
subjects. The pattern is roughly in accord with the typical Gauquelin
shape. Because the numbers involved are low, the pattern is inevitably

rough. Out of the possible 16 patterns a further 5 show the lopsided cross corresponding to a 'Gauquelin pattern'. Appendix 5 contains the patterns obtained from:

> Jupiter for high E scorers
> Mars for high P scorers
> Jupiter for high P scorers
> Saturn for high N scorers
> Jupiter for high L scorers
> Mars for high E scorers

Each has some appearance of the lopsided cross oriented so that sectors 1 and 4 contain peaks with minor peaks in sectors 7 and 10. The pattern emerges more clearly if the results from all these six distributions are pooled. Here the resemblance to the standard Gauquelin pattern is quite striking. However, there could still be some doubt about the authenticity of the result because, in effect, 6 of the 16 distributions have been selected. The crucial test comes when this result is compared with a result obtained by exactly the same process, but using the lowest 10%.

It was noted in Chapter 2 that Gauquelin found his professionals not only tended towards having appropriate planets prominent, but they also avoided inappropriate planets. Thus, generals had Mars prominent (peaks in sectors 1, 4, 7 and 10) but had the Moon distributed so that troughs appeared in sectors 1, 4, 7 and 10. (The Moon was found appropriate for writers but not for generals.)

If indeed, the patterns of peaks and troughs for certain top scorers and planets among the time twin subjects are genuine, then the lowest scorers should show troughs where the top scorers show peaks and vice versa. In Appendix 5 is shown first the pattern from the low scorers and then this same pattern with that from the high scorers superimposed on it. It can be seen that the peaks of one pattern do coincide with the troughs of the other. It can be concluded that the time twin subjects do conform with the 'Gauquelin rules'. There is particular corroboration in that the planetary indications do correspond with the psychological traits as found from the E, N, P and L scores.

- Extroversion is expected from Jupiter and to some extent Mars
- Psychotic tendencies are expected from Mars
- Neuroticism is expected from Saturn
- Tendencies towards self delusion are expected from Jupiter

The EPQ test was not designed to pick up specific planetary attributes but to measure certain described personality traits. Thus, it cannot be expected that there will be a one-to-one correspondence between a trait and a planet. A different sort of questionnaire would be needed to tease out individual planetary attributes. However, the EPQ has the great advantage that it has been extensively tested among many groups of subjects, and has also been checked for repeatability (extent to which a subject generates the same scores when tested at six month intervals). Furthermore the underlying variation of the scores with age and sex is known (quite modest effects). Overall, the EPQ is a very suitable tool for this investigation.

Conclusion

In the next chapter, the 'qualitative' part of the time twins project is described. In this chapter, all of the quantitative part has been described – the inception, the design, the collection of data, the results, the analysis and the interpretation. The time twins project has not 'proved astrology true' – that will take a great deal more data collection and analysis, if indeed it can ever be done on traditional astrology. There is a much larger fraction of traditional astrology waiting for any sort of quantitative justification than the fraction which has received support from quantitative research.

What the time twins project has done is to supply support for two tenets of 'twentieth century astrology'. Professional astrologers, since the Gauquelin results were accepted, have had to modify their views about the traditional 'weakness' of the cadent houses. The astrological teaching academies have had to incorporate the Gauquelin findings. Thus, twentieth century astrology is somewhat different from that of earlier centuries. The time twins project has furnished support for:

1. The notion that 'time twins' (close resemblers born with a small time separation) exist at all – and are not simply coincidences which have been singled out by journalists.

2. The 'Gauquelin rules' do have some application to 'ordinary people'. The main Gauquelin research results have concerned top professionals, and commentators have pointed out that there is no necessary inference that the same rules apply to 'ordinary people'.

There are additional points which have emerged from the project. Quite specific methods have been needed to tease out the significance of the results. Using average scores showed nothing of interest. It was necessary to seek the exceptional. The proportion of close resemblers (exceptionals) turned out to be substantially higher among those pairs with small birth time separations than those born far apart in time. Similarly, only by using the extreme EPNL scores from the personality tests could the Gauquelin patterns be found.

It seems almost certain that close resembling time twins are unusual in the general population – no higher than 10% and probably lower than this figure. Furthermore, this low incidence is an additional indicator of what can be called the 'star born' phenomenon. A certain proportion of the population, the star born, evince characteristics which are appropriate to the planetary pattern at their births. Gauquelin found a way of sifting his subjects so that the proportion of star born was higher than in a random sample. He did this by choosing the 'top people'. For reasons about which we can speculate there appear to be more star born among the high fliers than among ordinary people. There seems to be no good reason why the star born should be confined to the top professionals, and it is likely that asking for volunteers to help with an astrological research project is a way of finding more star born than would be found from a random sample. (It was noted that Dr Steffert's test with a larger random sample produced less corroboration of the Gauquelin rules than the time twins project sample – presumably because her sample contained a smaller proportion of star born.)

Finally, it must be emphasised that no single astrological experiment can be regarded as a reliable research block until it has been independently replicated. What the time twins project has shown is that this particular research technique has the potential to discover more about basic astrological truths. This is no mean feat. Dean attests to an immense amount of research effort which has come to nothing. Because it is convenient to collect birth dates for particular groups, there have been many attempts to demonstrate the truth of Sun-sign astrology. For example, there ought to be lots of Sun in Aries for military men and similar correspondences – but these expectations are dashed. The vast majority of astrological research endeavours have foundered. What is needed are some clear guidelines on what to look for. Gauquelin left a fine set of trails to follow, but his indications for research among 'ordinary people' were sparse. In the time twins project are some good guidelines for designing new experiments that are likely to succeed. Particularly likely to succeed is a straight replication of this project.

Chapter 5

Time Twins' Personalities

The last chapter dealt with the main time twins project: deciding on the 'target days', advertising for subjects who were born on one of those days and asking each of them to complete a psychological questionnaire. After analysis of the questionnaires we could see to what extent those subjects who were born close together in time were also close together psychologically. It emerged that there was a much higher proportion of 'close resemblers' among those separated by less than an hour than among those separated by four hours or more. Indeed, one could draw a graph showing the fall-off of 'resemblance' as the time separation of the births became greater

The project was directed primarily at discovering the existence of the 'time twin effect' but it was possible to check for further evidence of any astrological indications. Michel Gauquelin demonstrated that certain personality traits in his subjects were associated with specific prominent planets in their birth charts. Gauquelin's work was nearly all with eminent people, but clearly it would be of great interest to know whether his findings would apply to 'ordinary people'. The data we collected in the project could be used to test whether the 'Gauquelin planetary characteristics' showed up in our time twin subjects.

Despite the limited nature of the psychological questionnaire (measuring only extroversion, neuroticism, psychoticism and the tendency towards self-deception) we found that the same patterns of planetary distribution that Gauquelin had discovered were present for our time twin subjects.

Each of these discoveries is of great interest to researchers – who seek constantly for ingenious ways of putting questions to Nature (or 'devising good experiments' as we would say). However, in pursuing the statistics, we seem to have lost the rich tapestry of life. The subjects are living, breathing people, not collections of psychological variables. What about all those remarkable 'coincidences' which were described in the case studies of Chapter 1? In particular, is there any evidence to confirm astrologers' beliefs that the pattern of a person's life is influenced astro-logically? Gauquelin attempted to discover whether any of the big life events for his subjects were similarly timed when the subjects' births were separated by a short interval. He found nothing significant, but then he had quite a small sample of time twins on which to draw. In the project, we have enough close time twins to test whether there is any 'life pattern effect'.

The Interviews

There is a great temptation when collecting evidence for time twin effects to list the good cases (remarkable similarities) and also to dwell on the similarities themselves while ignoring those features which do not show any special likenesses. This is what happens in newspaper reports – after all, it makes a better story! However, if one is to obtain an unbiased result, then there must be no suppression of 'inconvenient data' – all data must be given equal weight. Thus, if one is going to interview the subjects then *all* the members of any chosen class must be included.

  The interview part of the project was carried out by selecting one of the six days and inviting all the subjects born on that day to be interviewed. It could be argued that all the subjects from each of the days should have been interviewed but the sheer logistic problems of such an undertaking loom large. In fact 14 November 1948 was chosen for the following reasons:

1. The subjects born in 1948 were now 44 years old – they had lived long enough for 'things to have happened to them'. Subjects born in 1964 (our earliest chosen year) have had that much less experience.

2. It was good to choose a day for which we had lots of replies (to provide a sizeable sample). Additionally, there was the risk that only a proportion of all the subjects who had completed questionnaires would also be willing to be interviewed. In the event only about a half of those who were invited to be interviewed actually agreed. There were about twice as many original replies for 14 November 1948 as for any other of the chosen days.

There were 17 subjects from 14 November 1948 who agreed to be interviewed. An interview form covering many aspects of their lives was prepared and used rigorously at each encounter, i.e., only those questions appearing on the form were asked and only replies responding to those questions were recorded. This was done in order to avoid 'hunting for similarities'. A copy of the interview form appears in Appendix 3. All kinds of items are thought by astrologers to be influenced, for example, physical appearance. So that you can decide whether any one of the facets recorded is relevant, a table has been prepared for all 17 subjects. This table appears on the next five pages. The order of appearance in the table is arbitrary but the subjects have been numbered to facilitate reference. There is, therefore, no reason to expect that subjects appearing next to each other in the table are close together in birth time. There is about the same ratio between the sexes as in the whole sample (⅓ men to ⅔ women).

The replies have been shortened to accommodate them in the table and the answers to certain questions do not appear (simply because there was no difference across the entire group: e.g., to the question 'What major illnesses have you had?', the universal answer was 'None').

Now, there are some time twins present in the table – there are pairs here who were born within quite a short time of each other. Without looking to see the answers, see if you can spot the time twins. Of course, you first have to decide which items of information are important . . .

	No. 1 (f)	No. 2 (f)
Present occupation	Midwife	Insurance broker
Past occupation	Teacher	Secretary
Desired occupation	Singer	Teacher
Date of marriage(s)	'83	'68
Births of children	'84, '87	'71, '74, '77
Hobbies/interests	Photography, singing	Cancer res. committee
Sports played	Athletics, swimming	Netball, swimming
Pet or pets	Dogs and cats	_____
Favourite author	George Orwell	_____
Instrument(s) played	Guitar, piano, organ	_____
Preferred music	W. African & Welsh choirs	Popular
Foreign travel	Extensive	Some

Most notable success	Excep. promotion at 21	Raising family
Most memorable event	Coming to England	Leaving home to work

	No. 3 (m)	No. 4 (m)
Present occupation	Motor mechanic	AA patrolman
Past occupation	Same	Auto electrician
Desired occupation	Same	Entertainer
Date of marriage(s)	'72 – '77, '86	'74
Births of children	'88	'79, '81
Hobbies/interests	Photography, motor cycles	DIY
Sports played	Badminton, cycling	_____
Pet or pets	Cat	_____
Favourite author	_____	_____
Instrument(s) played	_____	Guitar
Preferred music	Pop '60s, '70s	Country & Western
Foreign travel	Ext. (holidays)	Little
Most notable success	Self employment	_____
Most memorable event	Starting own business	TV talent contest

	No. 5 (m)	No. 6 (f)
Present occupation	Manager	Child minder
Past occupation	Rising to manager	Legal secretary
Desired occupation	Ship's captain	Teacher (young children)
Date of marriage(s)	'76	'70 - '88
Births of children	_____	'76, '83
Hobbies/interests	Current affairs	Sewing, tap dancing
Sports played	Rugby football	_____
Pet or pets	_____	Cat
Favourite author	_____	Thomas Hardy
Instrument(s) played	_____	_____
Preferred music	Opera	Classical
Foreign travel	V. ext. (holidays)	Little
Most notable success	Professional	_____
Most memorable event	Death of mother	Births of children

	No. 7 (m)	No. 8 (f)
Present occupation	Software consultant	Dispensing chemist
Past occupation	Computing	Same
Desired occupation	Professional musician	Academic
Date of marriage(s)	'71	'68
Births of children	'75, '77	'69
Hobbies/interests	Gardening, sci-fi	Theatre, reading
Sports played	Swimming	____
Pet or pets	____	Cats
Favourite author	____	Colbin Dexter
Instrument(s) played	Clarinet (amat. orch.)	____
Preferred music	Classical, Opera	Cole Porter
Foreign travel	V. ex. (wk related)	Little
Most notable success	1st class degree	Retn. to coll. at 30
Most memorable event	11+ exam. Gtng. marr.	Leaving school

	No. 9 (f)	No. 10 (f)
Present occupation	____	PA
Past occupation	(Diverse jobs)	Secretary
Desired occupation	With people	____
Date of marriage(s)	'71 – '73	'83
Births of children	____	'84, '88
Hobbies/interests	Antiques, dancing	Art, photography
Sports played	Tennis, badminton	Squash, badminton
Pet or pets	Breeds & shows dogs, cats	3 cats, 2 dogs
Favourite author	Evelyn Waugh	Clive James
Instrument(s) played	Guitar	Piano
Preferred music	Baroque	Vaughan Williams
Foreign travel	Extensive	Very extensive
Most notable success	Pet show 1st	Children
Most memorable event	Leaving Uruguay	Death of father

	No. 11 (f)	No. 12 (f)
Present occupation	Nursery nurse teacher	Care assistant
Past occupation	Nursery nurse	Accounts clerk
Desired occupation	Same	Caring role
Date of marriage(s)	'70 – '80 (partner)	'68 – '72, '74 – '91

		'73, '74, '82
Births of children	____	'73, '74, '82
Hobbies/interests	Theatre, FOE	Walking, reading
Sports played	Swimming	Swimming
Pet or pets	Many & varied	Dog, rabbit
Favourite author	____	Stephen King
Instrument(s) played	____	Piano
Preferred music	Folk, pop	Beethoven
Foreign travel	Ext. (work related)	Little
Most notable success	In teaching role	____
Most memorable event	40th birthday	Births of children

	No. 13 (m)	No. 14 (f)
Present occupation	Computing	____
Past occupation	Medical student	Secretary
Desired occupation	Author	Counselling
Date of marriage(s)	'76	'70 – '76
Births of children	'78, '82, '84	____
Hobbies/interests	Furniture making	Cooking, sewing
Sports played	____	Swimming
Pet or pets	Cats	____
Favourite author	Herman Hesse	____
Instrument(s) played	Piano	____
Preferred music	Classical	Middlebrow
Foreign travel	Little	Little
Most notable success	Family	____
Most memorable event	Abandoning medicine	Becoming 21

	No. 15 (f)	No. 16 (f)
Present occupation	Estate agent	Teacher
Past occupation	Secretary	Same
Desired occupation	Textile design	Dentist
Date of marriage(s)	'69	'71
Births of children	'71, '72, '76	'74, '76
Hobbies/interests	Flower arranging	Hill walking
Sports played	Golf, sailing	(School teams)
Pet or pets	Dog	____
Favourite author	____	Margaret Drabble
Instrument(s) played	____	____

Preferred music	Country & Western	Classical
Foreign travel	V. extensive	Little
Most notable success	Family	In teaching role
Most memorable event	Births of children	Getting married

No. 17 (f)

Present occupation	Prof. bassoon player
Past occupation	Teaching instrument
Desired occupation	Ballet dancer
Date of marriage(s)	'69 – '70, '79 – '91
Births of children	'81, '82
Hobbies/interests	Theatre, aerobics
Sports played	Jogging
Pet or pets	____
Favourite author	____
Instrument(s) played	Bassoon, piano
Preferred music	Classical & baroque
Foreign travel	Ext. (work related)
Most notable success	Playing professionally
Most memorable event	1st playing job

I hope that you tried to spot the twins first, because the coincidences always look much better with hindsight! Below are listed the birth times of the interviewee subjects in order from the earliest to the latest and accompanied by the numbers which identify them in the table.

Birth time	Number
00.05	10
00.30	12
01.00	8
04.00	1
05.00	11
05.30	9
06.15	13
07.00	6
08.00	15
08.00	17
08.15	7
09.00	16

09.20	3
12.00	5
12.15	2
22.00	4
23.00	14

With knowledge of the Gauquelin results one could expect that the main feature which should stand out when the time twin effect is being scrutinised is profession. The first thing that strikes one about these subjects' occupations is the large proportion of those in the 'caring' professions. In order from the earliest born there are:

    Care assistant
    Dispenser
    Nursery nurse teacher
    Child minder
    Midwife

To which could reasonably be added No. 13 who trained as a doctor and abandoned his training when just about to qualify, and also No. 16 whose desire (thwarted) was to become a dentist, plus No. 14 who would have become a counsellor. Slightly more remote is No. 2 whose dominant personal interest is serving on a cancer research committee.

It is difficult to be sure whether this high proportion of 'carers' is significant statistically because carers are drawn preponderantly from this stratum of society (those who write letters and take interest in research projects). Ignoring this bias, the proportion actually in caring posts is 5/17 = 29%. Taking all doctors, nurses, therapists, paramedics, child minders, care workers, dispensers, nursery nurses, it would be difficult to reach even 5% of the work force. To find 5 out of 17 in a sample is unlikely – about 1 in 1,000. However, this figure should not be regarded as more than suggestive because of the bias effect noted earlier. There is some interest attached to these chosen professions because it accords well with astrologers' beliefs that carers are drawn from the water signs (Cancer, Scorpio and Pisces). Our subjects all have Sun in Scorpio. It is unusual to find any evidence for the Sun signs so this should not be overlooked!

To add to the water sign association, no fewer than 6 of the interviewees name swimming as their sport: Nos. 1, 2, 7, 11, 12 and 14.

The Pairs

There are 18 potential pairs separated by 1 hour or less:

Nos.	Minutes apart
10-12	25
10-8	55
12-8	30
11-1	60
11-9	30
13-9	45
13-6	45
6-15	60
6-17	60
15-17	0
15-7	15
17-7	15
7-16	45
15-16	60
17-16	60
16-3	20
5-2	15
4-14	60

The Bassoonist and the Clarinettist

Taking profession and desired profession as the likeliest source of resemblances we have one striking pair: 17-7. No. 17 (female) is a professional bassoonist and No. 7 (male) is an enthusiastic amateur clarinettist (playing in amateur orchestras) who, given the option of an alternative career, would have been a professional musician. These are the only two 'serious' musicians in the collection of 17 subjects. There are 6 others who play instruments (3 piano, 3 guitar) primarily for recreation.

To find two serious woodwind players in such a small collection is remarkable but note that they were born 15 minutes apart. This is the most striking pair, because of the sheer rarity of professional or semi-professional woodwind players.

The Animal Lovers

No. 11 and No. 9 (both female) stand out as the animal lovers. Whereas many of the others neither have nor want pets of any kind, these two have an enthusiasm for animals which would be unusual in any company; No. 9 with most of the ground floor of her house used for keeping cats and dogs (some of them prize winners at shows) and No. 11 with the most remarkable assortment of pets that one could expect to encounter.

The contrast with most of the others is striking. It was commonplace to hear that 'dogs and cats leave hair all over the furniture' (which is true but of no importance if you really like keeping a pet).

Business

There are two members of the collection who, unlike the others, are involved in business. No. 5 is a manager in a large organisation (for which he has worked throughout his career). No. 2 is an insurance broker (taking up a business career after raising a family).

The distribution of birth times for the interviewees is far from uniform. There is a high concentration during the morning (10 between 4.00 and 9.20) then a break until two at 12.00 and 12.15 with the two at 22.00 and 23.00 bringing up the rear. Our business pair are the noon children, with 15 minutes separating them.

There would be nothing remarkable about finding two business executives from the population at large (they are much commoner than bassoonists!) The point here is that these are the only two in the collection.

Hobbies, Authors and Music

Only two interviewees named 'reading' as one of their principle interests and they are a 'pair' – No. 12 and No. 8.

Only two interviewees named purely domestic interests: 'cooking and sewing' in the one case, 'DIY' in the other, and these are the latest born pair – Nos. 4 and 14.

Only 8 of the 17 named a favourite author and 5 of those chose authors who could be regarded as 'serious' reading (George Orwell, Evelyn Waugh, Thomas Hardy and Margaret Drabble). Of these 5, there are 3 who were chosen by members of pairs – Nos. 9 and 13 plus Nos. 13 and 6. This would not be remarkable except for the fact that these same three (Nos. 9, 13 and 6) account for one of the clusters of classical music. There are two other classical music clusters – Nos. 10, 12 and Nos. 17, 7, 16. An additional similarity is that Nos. 10 and 12 both play the piano.

Successes and Notable Events

'Greatest success' and 'most notable event' are generally unremarkable, being mainly concerned with marriage, family, births of children, leaving home, death of a parent or a particular birthday.

Just one or two stand out. The most striking are Nos. 17 and 7. No. 17 (the bassoonist) is concerned very much with career and names 'playing professionally' as greatest success and 'first playing job' as most notable event. Similarly No. 7 names 'getting 1st class degree' as greatest success and 'passing 11+' as most notable event.

Clusters of Similarity

In order to see the interesting clusters which have been described above, a table (5.1) has been constructed on p.64 showing just the 6 categories (Hobby/interest, Favourite author, Instrument played, Preferred music, Greatest success, Most notable event) for each interviewee in birth time order.

Where there are 'coincidences' and the pairs have birth times within an hour of each other, rings have been drawn enclosing the coincidences. The interesting feature of these rings is the way in which they concentrate. Out of 13 rings only 3 occur in isolation (12-8 'reading', 4-14 'DIY and cooking/sewing' and 7-16 'classical music'). 6 rings occur in 'doubles', i.e. there are two coincidences affecting each time twin pair (10-12, 9-13 and 13-6). Finally, there are 4 rings affecting just one time twin pair. This last set of coincidences applies to No. 7 and 17. Their woodwind playing has already been noted, but additionally they share taste in music and have the same views about career and professional success. One final point about them which does not appear in the table – they have both travelled extensively on work-related trips. (Only 3 of all the interviewees' travel is work related and 2 of the 3 are the woodwind players, though their travel is for different purposes).

'Failures'

There are 18 pairs born close together from the collection and only one of these pairs shows a set of striking similarities. Of the remainder, there are

No	Hobby	Favourite author	Instrument	Music	Success	Notable event
10	Art Photography	Clive James	Piano	Vaughan Williams	Children	Death of father
12	Walking Reading	Stephen King	Piano	Beethoven	—	Births of children
8	Theatre Reading	Colbin Dexter	—	Cole Porter	Return to college	Leaving school
1	Photography Sewing	George Orwell	Guitar Piano	Choirs	Promotion at 21	Coming to England
11	Theatre FoE	—	—	Folk Pop	Teaching role	40th birthday
9	Antiques Dancing	Evelyn Waugh	Guitar	Baroque	Pet show 1st prize	Leaving Uraguay
13	Furniture making	Herman Hesse	Piano	Classical	Family	Leaving medicine
6	Sewing Tap dancing	Thomas Hardy	—	Classical	—	Births of children
15	Flower arranging	—	—	Country & Western	Family	Births of children
17	Theatre Aerobics	—	Bassoon Piano	Classical Baroque	Playing profess.	First playing job
7	Gardening Sci-fi	—	Clarinet	Classical Opera	1st class degree	11+ Marriage
16	Hill walking	Margaret Drabble	—	Classical	Teaching role	Marriage
3	Photography Motor cycles	—	—	Pop – '60s '70s	Self-employed	Owning business
5	Current affairs	—	—	Opera	Professional	Death of Σmother
2	Cancer committee	—	—	Popular	Raising family	Leaving home
4	DIY	—	Guitar	Country & Western	—	TV talent contest
14	Cooking sewing	—	—	Middle-brow	—	Becoming 21

Fig. 5.1

two that merit choice and a handful of 'coincidences' which are interesting, but the collection does not give support to the notion that all pairs of time twins are close resemblers.

Photographs were taken of each of the interviewees. Independent observers were asked to note any physical resemblances between any pair from the collection. There were no clear physical resemblances apparent. The likely conclusion is that physical resemblance among time twins is quite rare. It has been noted in some of the spectacular cases which reach the newspapers but is perhaps down at the 1 in 1,000 level or lower. Additionally, each interviewee was asked to write his or her forename as they would for a signature. There were no noticeable similarities of style.

The cases reported in newspapers often have the same forenames. The following forenames occurred in our collection of 17 interviewees:

Antoinette	Graham	Martin
Barbara	Helen	Mary
David	Janet	Sandra
David	Jean	Susan
George	Maggie	Vanessa
Gillian	Marilyn	

There are two Davids in the collection, and they were not born close together in time. Even those with slightly similar names (Mary, Martin, Marilyn) were not born near each other in time. Maybe, like physical similarity, this sort of correspondence is rare.

One of the tenets of traditional astrology has been the timing of life events from the birth chart by the use of 'transits' and 'directions'.[1] These are technical terms whose meaning is not important in this context. Suffice it to say that the life event indications should be the same for two individuals born at the same time. Astrologers would argue that precision of birth time is crucial for obtaining accurate prediction of life events. However, one might have expected some correspondence between the events occurring in the lives of the interviewees.

All but one of the interviewees have been married, three of them more than once. Do time twins tend to marry in the same year? Well, one has to be careful about drawing any conclusions because people do tend to marry in the same period of their lives. You would expect that a majority of people born in 1948 to have married between 1968 and 1978. Indeed, 14 out of the 16 first marriages were during this decade. Below are the years of marriage and the interviewees who were married in that year:

Year	Interviewee
68	2, 8, 12
69	15, 17
70	6, 14
71	7, 9, 16
72	3
73	
74	4, 12
75	
76	5, 13
77	
78	
79	17
80	
81	
82	
83	1, 10

(and No. 3 in 86)

There are just 3 of the 18 pairs of time twins who were married in the same year: 8-12; 15-17; 7-16.

The probability of no time twins marrying in the same year = .13
The probability of 1 pair of time twins marrying in the same year = .35
The probability of 2 pairs of time twins marrying in the same year = .27
The probability of 3 or more pairs marrying in the same year = .17

I.e. the chance is about 5 to 1 against finding 3 of our time twins marrying in the same year. This is not very convincing.

What about the births of their children? Altogether there are 28 children born to the interviewees (so far). There were 16 possibilities for time twins to have been parents of children who were born in the same year. Of these the only coincidences are:

Nos. 6 and 15 had a child in '76
Nos. 15 and 16 had a child in '76

(Neither of these pairs were married in the same year.)

Again we have to say that there is nothing remarkable about this result.

Finally, there is the possibility that other life events besides marriage and the births of children would show up coincidences. The interviewees were asked to name and date the most significant events which had happened to them, but many of these occurrences were in the category of 'programmed events' – leaving school, leaving home, graduating; or else they were marriage/births of children. One or two events fell outside these groups but they do not show up as corresponding between time twins, i.e. same type of occurrence in same year.

Clearly, there is no firm evidence from this study to suggest that time twins show any similar patterns in the events of their lives. This does not rule out the possibility. Among the reported cases of strikingly similar time twins there have been notable coincidences in life events.

Conclusion

The striking coincidences to emerge from this closer look at some of the time twins in the sample suggest that profession, desired profession and interests are the areas in which similarities associated with small differences in birth time manifest themselves. There is no firm evidence to indicate that physical appearance, forename or the pattern of life events are associated between pairs of time twins.

Although this result is disappointing, it is worth noting that the accordance with the Gauquelin findings continues:

1. He scored his greatest successes when dealing with collections of people who shared the same profession.

2. He sought correspondences between important events occurring in the lives of those pairs in his collections who were born close together in time and failed to find any.

3. The area of his second impressive research finding concerned personality traits – and the psychological factors making up personality have turned out to be the best evidence emerging from this time twins project.

Once again, it must be pointed out that the failure to find more spectacular 'coincidences' in this study (and also in the Gauquelin work) is likely to derive from the progressive rarity of items such as close physical resemblance, identical names and synchronised life events. The reason for putting this argument is that the reported cases contain all of the resemblance material found in this study *plus* the additional items of physical resemblance etc. Thus, the likely reason for failure to find the additional items in this study is simply because the sample size is small, whereas the reported cases in newspapers are drawn from very large samples (virtually the whole populations of countries).

It is unsatisfactory to leave this argument about extreme resemblances as essentially a conjecture, but it must be appreciated that any research project to establish a factual basis for the conjecture would entail extremely large samples and become, for all practical purposes, out of the question.

Chapter 6

Time Twins and Astrology

Have we Proved Astrology True?

Modern science shuns the word 'truth'. The contemporary view is that we have a set of theories which are essentially provisional hypotheses and these hypotheses can be modified – or indeed abandoned – if fresh evidence appears which contradicts the current paradigm.

This thoroughly pragmatic approach has been forced on us by the radical changes in paradigm that have occurred at intervals over the past century. Relativity and quantum theory are such profound breaks with tradition that it would be absurd to suppose that they are the 'final' version of truth and not to be modified again.

However, these unsettling changes present a false picture to those who look at science from the 'outside'. From the inside, the picture looks different. The analogy I prefer is that of a group of archaeologists trying to assemble a building which, they assume, existed in the past. The fragments are littered over the ground and it needs a lot of imagination to perceive that there is order among all the sherds. Not all the parts of the building have yet been uncovered and they are not sure how much still remains to be found. There are some bold spirits who make heroic assumptions and declare that some group of blocks which they have identified represent the main structure, the outlines of which enable them to use lots more of the fragments to fill up gaps and demonstrate a convincing form. It is even possible for them occasionally to predict that such and such a fragment of this shape and size will be found to fit a gap in their construction. When the piece is indeed found, the successful prediction is hailed as a triumph and a confirmation that the original design from which the prediction could be made was sound and can continue to be used. From time to time, it becomes clear that some group of pieces simply will not fit the current proposed design and a radical rethink is needed to accommodate them. Sometimes it is necessary to accept that the main columns of the previous design are no more than 'curtain' walling – they are just the façade of a much more fundamental structure underlying the one which had been thought to be the main edifice.

Now, the point of this analogy is that it emphasises the need to accommodate all the previous findings. We do not simply reach for a fresh sheet of paper, and design a new theory. Large parts of the building remain remarkably untouched. To illustrate this point, consider the fact that after nearly a century since the acceptance of relativity, the nautical almanac is compiled using just Newtonian mechanics. The deviations from Newton which relativity entails are so small that errors generated by ignoring them are negligible.

It is true that some paradigm shifts are so spectacular that older researchers cannot adjust to them. The quantum theory was quite shocking to physicists over forty. But this change was really no worse than the archaeologists discovering that what they had thought was hard stone turns out to be no more than dried mud. The whole structure suddenly looks insubstantial – a flimsy affair. Quantum theory hinted at great gaps in certainty opening up in the firm everyday world. Einstein[1] could declare that he did not believe that God was playing at dice with us – but he was just showing his prejudices.

The analogy holds even further than described above. The archaeologists have to believe that there was a building for them to discover. As Rupert Sheldrake[2] remarks, scientists have to have faith in the existence of 'laws' for them to discover. If the universe were just the form presented by the capricious play of blind random forces, all the patterns and regularities 'discovered' by scientists would be just occasional flukes without substance.

One last analogy: if an archaeologist is convinced that what he is looking at is the remains of a bath house and it is actually a place where food was stored, he will make slow progress. If you get stuck in the wrong mind set, you will not discover interesting things. You will go on trying to fit inconvenient fragments into the form you have convinced yourself is real and true.

The successful practice of scientific discovery requires a curious mixture of humility and arrogance. If you do not have enough humility just to look clearly and wonderingly at the raw material you will not find anything. On the other hand, unless you have the sheer arrogance, at the end, to say that you do understand it, and it all fits together like this and this . . . then you will have been just another stamp collector.

The reason for this discussion about science is the need to place astrological research in context. What are we doing? Are we trying to prove astrology true? Now, the idea of a researcher 'trying to prove anything true' is very worrying. Whereas, if I said that we are trying to fit some more pieces into this reconstruction of a building, that would be much nearer the mark. It is particularly difficult in astrology to look clearly and wonderingly and without prejudice, because there is a great mass of writings claiming to be 'the truth' and, whether you like it or not, the influence of those writings on your thinking is powerful. If you have a lot of faith in the writings then you may go on chasing one of the 'well known truths' only to admit in the end that it has been a fruitless quest. The researchers who gathered masses of data to 'prove' the validity of the Sun signs were, as far as we can see, wasting their time. In contrast, researchers prepared to follow up a lead, even if it is flat contrary to the received wisdom, have been rewarded. Gauquelin discovered that the important locations for his prominent planets were the 'cadent' houses of the chart. (Houses 1, 4, 7, 10 are the 'angular' houses; numbers 2, 5, 8 and 11 are the 'succedent' houses; numbers 3, 6, 9, 12 are the 'cadent' houses. But note that the 'sectors' he used were numbered in the reverse order to that of the houses.) The cadent houses have traditionally been the weak houses.

The Time Twins Project and other Astrological Research

It is appropriate to ask how the time twins project has aided 'construction of the building' – how the findings fit in with preceding research.

1. *Paucity*

The first striking feature about the time twins findings is that they confirm the Gauquelin results in respect of elusiveness. When he started, Michel had to use quite special collections (his top flight professionals) to get results at all. Even then, the actual proportions of cases that showed 'appropriate planets' were quite modest. Given large samples, even small deviations from expected turned out to be significant, but that does not alter the fact that the effect he found was in a real sense 'elusive'.

Similarly, the fraction of time twins who bear close psychological resemblances to one another is quite small. (We have to hunt to find them.) The same applies when we are looking for other resemblances in their interests and their lives. Closely similar time twins are not common.

2. *The Cadent Houses*

The point was made earlier that Gauquelin, having discovered the cadent houses as the preferred location of prominent planets, pursued this line through a variety of professions and then several different countries. The time twins research has shown that indeed the same patterns of planet occurrence appear for the psychological 'extreme value' subjects. This is all the more notable in that confirmation of an effect which contradicts traditional belief requires more demonstration than for an effect already receiving credence. (This point is often made by sceptics in their reference to astrology. Thus a critic will say: 'Because astrology is inherently so improbable, it would require a mass of evidence, showing very high significance levels, for anyone to take it seriously.')

3. *Profession and Personality*

Astrologers maintain that astrology applies to just about everything you can think of in respect of a person's life. Gauquelin's success occurred in two areas: profession and personality. His greatest triumph lay in the findings for groups of professionals and his next best result was for their personality traits. (They are put in that order, because there have recently been some queries about the procedure which he used when selecting adjectives from his subjects' biographies. There is at least a possibility that conscious or unconscious bias was present in his selections. Suitbert Ertel[3] has raised this question and attempted to repeat some of Gauquelin's work using students to make the same selections. He reports that they do not replicate the Gauquelin findings.) It might be argued that Gauquelin did not look at other facets of individuals' lives, but a close reading of his work indicates that he tried out many of the supposed effects which are described in text books on astrology. He was, for example, unsuccessful in finding any tie-up with life events except for a small but just significant indication that the time of death[4] accorded with the same locations of appropriate prominent planets as occurred at birth (for 4,000 random subjects born in Paris).

Similarly, the time twins research indicated that profession (plus interests) and psychological traits associate significantly with their astrological indicators, but all attempts to find other factors (life events, physical characteristics etc.) were unsuccessful.

This is not to argue that the other traditional beliefs of astrology are without foundation, but rather to suggest that they must apply much more weakly than the ones which have emerged from research to date. It is interesting to note that among the reported cases of time twins there are some pairs for whom the additional resemblances (beyond those to be expected from our research findings) extend to physical similarity, forenames and many life events such as time of marriage, births of children and even cause/time of death. This hints that there is a ranking of features, with profession and personality heading the order, coincident appearance/name at the next level and life events coinciding as the rarest phenomenon to be encountered.

Development of Astrological Research

Our picture of astrology has changed as research findings have been absorbed. Of course, the die-hard traditionalists have not been affected by research results. This is rather like fundamental Christians insisting on the literal truth of the Garden-of-Eden story long after the evidence for evolution spread over billions of years has been accepted by virtually everyone else. The early writers on astrology were as fallible as any biblical author and it is naive to take any of these writings on trust. (This is not the same as ignoring what has been written. Ignoring early beliefs is like throwing out the baby with the bathwater – there is a great treasure trove to be discovered – but a little scepticism is appropriate.)

Contemporary teaching of astrology has taken on much of the Gauquelin findings, particularly the power of angular planets – even though they be in the cadent houses. There is unwillingness to discard the outer planets despite Gauquelin's failure to find any association between prominent Uranus, Neptune or Pluto and expected chosen profession or personality traits. The opinion of modern astrologers tends towards the notion that more of traditional astrology could be demonstrated by researchers if sufficiently good experiments were devised. This position is justifiable, because Gauquelin himself 'discovered Venus' late in his researches. There was quite a long period in which the only mention, in his research accounts, was of Mars, Jupiter, Saturn and the Moon. Now, if Venus was found 'late', why should not Mercury and the outer planets be shown to have effects in due course when the researchers have 'caught up'?

The Future for Astrological Research

In the account of the time twins research, it was noted that the Eysenck Personality Questionnaire, though having several highly desirable features for the task, was a 'blunt tool' for investigating planetary characteristics. It is to be expected that among the range of personality types to be found will be individuals who exemplify all the richness evoked by reading the lists of adjectives found in Gauquelin's inventories (derived from his subjects' biographies). Scores on the E, N, P and L scales do not tell us about the degree to which a person is affable, charming, courteous, flattering, obliging or poetic (some of the adjectives found by Gauquelin to be associated with Venus). Why not use a questionnaire which actually attempts to place a person as a planetary type? Questionnaires whose results place the respondent in a multi-dimensional space already exist. For example, the Cattell 16 PF test attempts to measure 16 separate personality factors.[5]

A research group at the Urania Trust is attempting to design a questionnaire which will identify the extent to which a respondent is Venusian, Martian, Jupiterian or Saturnian. Indeed, because there is no good reason to ignore the other planets, the questionnaire will also attempt to measure the extent to which someone is Mercurial, Uranian, Neptunian or Plutonian and whether their personality reflects Solar or Lunar traits.

Although the project is in its early stages, there seems to be evidence from the first trials that the questions 'cluster' into groups corresponding to the individual planets, i.e. that there are strong correlations between answers to the questions within one planetary group, so that a person answering 'yes' to one question from a particular group will tend to answer 'yes' to other questions from the same group. This suggests that other scales can be used to assess personality besides those already used by psychologists. The universe of 'all possible questions' is a large one and it would be surprising if the standard psychological questionnaire covered all facets of it. What is much more likely is to find that people are spread out on an extroversion scale if you ask lots of questions intended to measure extroversion, whereas if you had asked lots of questions intended to measure Venusian qualities you would find them spread out on a 'Venusian scale'.

Even to demonstrate that the planetary qualities can be detected by means of a questionnaire is a worthwhile enterprise. Denis Elwell[6] in *Cosmic Loom* argues that if you look at everyday reality with an astrological eye you can see the threads of the planets woven into the fabric along different dimensions to those which we see ordinarily. This is a fascinating concept –

the idea that reality is shot through with quite other qualities than those which we decide to categorise. He offers as a striking example how the Saturnian theme shows through the way the element lead (traditionally the Saturn element) is a poison affecting ultimately the bones of the skeleton (Saturnian feature of the body). In turn the skeleton has always been a symbol of death and mortality – and time itself (Saturn again). The association with the past and also with structure has a further echo in modern science – the inexorable increase of entropy (loss of form and structure) with time. (Saturn is the planet of structure.) Finally, he points out that it is entirely fitting that the substance which resists this time decay most strongly is an isotope of lead: lead 204. 'Long before the earth's supply of lead 204 (4 trillion tons of it) has decayed, the sun will have burned itself out and the universe as we know it will have become something else.'

If, indeed, reality is shot through with planetary themes, then it could be confidently expected that people can be measured on planetary scales, though to be really convincing we would like to see a clear correlation between high values on, say, the Jupiter scale, from the questionnaire, and Jupiter prominent in the chart. It seems that even in the first small samples of their research the UT team have found some indications of correlation between planetary scores and planetary location in the cadent houses. It will be necessary to wait for more comprehensive tests to be mounted before we will know if this latest attempt to catch 'elusive astrology' in a statistical net has been successful.

A second research team at UT is attempting to replicate the experiment carried out by Fuzeau-Braesch[7] on distinguishing between fraternal twins which was described in Chapter 2.

Theories

It was remarked earlier that there are continuous attempts, in the scientific world, to put together theories which accommodate all of the experimental data. This has several advantages:

1. The theory will often enable a 'prediction' to be made of what will be found if such and such an observation is made. If that prediction turns out to be true then the theory has received useful support.

2. The theory will often suggest new lines of experimental investigation, and by this means the further development of experiment and theory creation is stimulated.

3. The theory may carry resonances of other (successful) theories and will thereby enjoy greater confidence that it is sound.

Gauquelin worked for some time on his own theory of 'the midwife planets'. The idea behind this theory was that a planet in a key location could stimulate a foetus into being born provided that certain specific traits were already inbuilt. The theory runs into difficulties when the gap between the onset of labour and the actual birth is taken into account. The gap is frequently many hours long and during this time the planets will have changed location significantly. However, the important time found from his researches was the birth time and not the time of labour onset.

Even if there had been no problem with the time of labour, the Gauquelin theory offered no clear physical link which could have operated. More recently, Seymour[8] has put forward a physical theory to explain the Gauquelin research findings. The basis of the Seymour theory is the way in which the planets can affect tidal movements in the magnetosphere surrounding the earth. Masses of charged particles streaming out of the sun are strongly influenced in their motion by magnetic fields and tides can develop within this motion. The strength of the tides depends on resonance, so that even quite modest influences such as the planets exert can result in the build up of appreciable tides. Changes in the magnetosphere are sensed as change in the geomagnetic strength here on earth. Furthermore, it is known that many creatures are sensitive to quite small changes in geomagnetic strength. Thus there is the possibility that the foetus could be affected in the same way. Gauquelin found that his heredity results were different on days when the geomagnetic strength was high compared with times when it was weak. Hence there is a possible connecting causal chain which could explain the source of the planetary correlations.

In *The Message of Astrology*[9] I have attempted to assemble a theory which could explain nearly all of the experimental data. Viewed from the citadel of orthodox science, my theory leans unacceptably on the existence of a 'soul' seeking an appropriate birth time. As such, it comes into the same category as Rupert Sheldrake's morphogenetic fields – to be shunned by orthodoxy until such time as there is other evidence to support it (because any theory conjuring up novel entities or novel fields is regarded as inherently implausible and thus requires much supporting evidence to be taken seriously).

However difficult it is to develop a theory which explains astrological research findings, the effort is essential, because otherwise there can be no confidence that the findings represent a real part of the structure of our universe. Without any 'thought-structure' to embed the experimental results into our world, they are just a collection of bizarre oddities – with no confidence that the findings could be replicated in further trials or that the patterns found would be stable over time. No amount of *ex cathedra* utterances on the ultimate truth of astrology is any substitute for experimental evidence supporting a consistent theory which lies within established scientific laws.

Conclusion

What is encouraging about current developments in astrological research is the way in which new lines are being pursued. Gauquelin left a monumental legacy. He showed how it was possible to make advances through rigorous statistical methods. The rift between himself and most practising astrologers was, in one sense, necessary. He had to eschew the easy path of reading the books and instead, work with the raw data. His reward was a tantalising glimpse of a new window on our universe. Astrology fits very badly within the existing scientific paradigm, and yet if we ignore 'inconvenient' facts, our vision is that much impaired – we will not gain those insights into the greater intricacies that lie beyond the orthodox scientific model.

Gauquelin's development is a fascinating story. He was led on from his early success with collections of outstanding professionals to attempt novel experiments branching out from the first examples. All the time he sought a physical explanation – that was why he followed up the idea of heredity playing a part and investigated the possibility of parents and their children sharing common prominent planets. That turned out to have an unexpected but revelatory outcome because after his first positive results he continued by probing whether intervention in the birth process would show any difference in the correlations. Indeed it did and if there was drastic intervention the patterns faded altogether as though the child was then 'born at the wrong time'. This result is profoundly contradictory of traditional teaching where the actual moment of birth, however influenced, is the crucial astrological time.

It is a classic case of an inspired researcher, driven by the self-imposed task of solving a puzzle with only the most tenuous of outlines – a puzzle which had defeated earlier researchers wielding the tool of statistics. Gauquelin has set a splendid example to the researchers who follow him. Persevering with the collection of data and being prepared to follow up leads suggested by his findings (even if there appeared contradictions of the traditional wisdom) he has opened up new vistas.

Similar bold spirits are needed now to push back the frontiers. As in all the best research, Gauquelin's findings raise as many questions as they answer. Who will discover why he could find no effects deriving from Uranus, Neptune or Pluto? What sort of experiments would demonstrate that the outer planets are at all relevant?

The other need is for more attempts to devise a satisfactory model that will explain the working of astrology. Elwell has conjured up a multi-dimensional world with the weft of astrology interwoven with the warp of the everyday world which is familiar to us. However, it is difficult to see how this picture can be developed into a full model with comprehensive explanatory power. Similarly, Seymour's physical model has a lot going for it, but it lacks explanatory power for many of the most intriguing effects emerging from contemporary research.

Currently, astrology is attractive to vast numbers of people who find its tenets mysterious, intriguing and implausible – but also satisfying to some intuitive faculty. These people do not want to probe into it: they want to believe that there really is truth in this ancient scheme. Only a few people have an inquiring stance, willing to discover whatever is there, and of those only a minority want anything to do with astrology. Thus, it is no surprise that little research of any value was conducted until the middle of this century. If more people knew that there has been successful research, that not only is there 'something in it' but parts of it are now well established, then there would be more volunteers to pick up the baton.

The concluding message is hope that, because the time twins project has yielded some support for the 'new astrology', more inquirers will tackle astrological research.

Appendix 1

Computation of the Natal Horoscope

First hand experience teaching Adult Education classes confirms that the majority of beginners find calculations the hardest facet of astrology to master. The terminology is foreign and easily confused and the calculations, while easy enough, nevertheless seem to include a constant stream of pitfalls all leading to simple mistakes. No matter how experienced an astrologer one may be it is easy to make errors in chart computation, but with practice the factors involved come to be seen as a sequence of simple and logical steps.

Accurate chart calculations are basic to astrology. Chart calculations require some expenditure – approximately £60.00 – and it is important to double check all workings time and time again. If one wishes to be a serious student of astrology one should accept as mandatory that one masters chart computation. If a beginner it is as well to use one of the many organisations offering computer calculation services listed at the end of this appendix.

Note: it is only advised that use be made of computer technology to compute the horoscope and not for interpretation; this should be undertaken by an experienced, respected and professional astrologer.

Reference Materials

Birth Data – time, date and place of birth. The more accurate the birth time the more correct the interpretation can be. The horoscope is a picture of the heavens at the moment of birth. Planets must be located with respect to the zodiac first and then with respect to the horizon. To do this accurately it is necessary to have the exact birth data.

(When the time is not known a Noon day chart can be set up, placing 0°

79

Aries on the Ascendant and inserting the planets at their noon day position as given in the Ephemeris. Houses are ignored completely.

The time of birth can be *rectified* using three or four known events that have occurred in the life of the individual, although rectification is a somewhat arbitrary and speculative means of assessing the birth times and should only be undertaken by an experienced astrologer.)

Time Changes – all birth times in astrology are corrected to Greenwich Mean Time (GMT) and a knowledge of time zones, daylight, wartime and summertime changes are required to correct birthtime to GMT. The selection of Time Changes books by Doris Doane, *Time Changes in the USA*, *Time Changes in Canada and Mexico* and *Time Changes in the World* are the most accurate and comprehensive compilations of these changes currently available.

World Atlas – the location of birth is required to determine the longitude and latitude of the birthplace. The *Times Atlas* is generally recommended.

The Ephemeris – booklet published annually and which contains the positions of the Sun, Moon and planets at noon Greenwich Mean Time (GMT) for every day of the year. Some publications give positions at midnight, *Raphael's Ephemerides* and the *Concise Planetary Ephemeris* are generally recommended.

Table of Houses – this is a small booklet of tables to which one may refer in order to find the sign and degree on the Ascendant and Midheaven (MC) which correspond to the local sidereal time at birth, for latitude of birthplace; *Raphael's Table of Houses in Northern Latitudes* and *Table of Houses in Great Britain* are recommended.

Blank birth chart forms (not essential)

Additional references – a good astrological textbook is suggested for additional guidance. Among the most widely used textbooks are *The Astrologer's Handbook* by Sakioan and Acker, *Teach Yourself Astrology* by Jeff Mayo and possibly *The Modern Textbook of Astrology* by M. E. Hone.

Stages In Computation

1. Determine the time of birth in *Greenwich Mean Time (GMT)*

2. Calculate the *Local Sidereal Time (LST)* at birth
3. Calculate the *Ascendant (ASC)* and *Midheaven (MC)* positions
4. Calculate the *Planetary Positions*
5. Calculate the *Planetary Aspects*

Points to remember:

- *Correct copying of figures* is essential. Make sure minutes and seconds are entered in the correct columns.
- Check the Ephemeris for any *change of zodiac* sign
- Calculations are based on the *sexagismal* system, which employs multiples of 60 rather than 10.
- Use of the *24 hour clock.*

It is advised that use be made of the standard forms on which explanation of the individual stages is given (reference Figure A1.1).

Stage 1: Determining the Time of Birth in Greenwich Mean Time (GMT)

The Ephemeris is based on GMT time and a given birthtime may require a correction using the Time Changes to GMT. Birth data may be given in GMT time, Summer Time, Double Summer Time, Zone or Standard Time or in births prior to 1880 by Local Mean Time. Where using zone or standard time (i.e. for births outside the United Kingdom) if the birthplace is *East* of Greenwich the difference is subtracted, if *West* of Greenwich the difference is added to convert to GMT.

Worked example Fig. A1.1: Prince Charles' birthdata as recorded 14 November 1948, London, at 9.14 p.m. Referring to the Atlas, London has a latitude of 51 °N 32' and a longitude of 00 °W 08'. Referring to the Time Changes of the World *there is no correction to the time as given which is 21.14 p.m. GMT.*

Stage 2: Calculating the Local Sidereal Time at Birth (LST)

The Local Sidereal Time (star time) is required to identify the Ascendant and Midheaven of the horoscope and to which houses the planets and zodiac signs will relate. Referring to the Ephemeris, look up the sidereal time for the day in question at Greenwich at noon or midnight depending on which tables you are using.

CALCULATION FOR LOCAL SIDEREAL TIME FOR GIVEN TIME
IN ORDER TO OBTAIN ASCENDANT AND MIDHEAVEN
BY DIRECT METHOD

FOR NORTHERN HEMISPHERE

1. Enter birth-date and place on form.
2. Find latitude and longitude from atlas.
3. Enter birth-time as given.
4. Convert to G.M.T. by adding or subtracting Zone standard. E —, W +.
5. If standard is G.M.T. enter as o hours.
   If summer time, subtract 1 hour, if double summer time, subtract 2 hours.
6. **Result is G.M.T.**
7. If conversion to G.M.T. has altered date, enter.
8. From ephemeris, take Sidereal Time at **Noon G.M.T.**, enter.
9. Enter hours and minutes TO or FROM Noon G.M.T.
   For a.m. birth, subtract, for p.m. **add** interval to S.T.
10. Calculate acceleration on interval (10 seconds for each hour).
    For a.m. birth subtract, for p.m. add to above result (No. 9).
11. **Result is Sidereal Time at Greenwich at birth.**
12. Find longitude equivalent in **time** by multiplying longitude by 4 and calling result minutes and seconds of time. Long W —. Long E +.
13. **Result is LOCAL SIDEREAL TIME AT BIRTH.**
14. Find Local Sidereal Time in Tables of Houses for given latitude to obtain degrees of Ascendant and Midheaven (M.C.).
    Chart according to system of house division used.

FOR SOUTHERN HEMISPHERE

(a) Add 12 hours to Local Sidereal Time of birth.
(b) Reverse signs. Example : For Cancer, read Capricorn.

STAGE 1	1. Birth-date ...		D M Y 14 NOV 1948
	Birth-place		LONDON
	2. Latitude ...		51 32 N
	Longitude ...		00 08 W
			h m s
	TIME :		
	3. Birth-time as given	*a.m., p.m.	21 14 00
	4. Zone Standard	*E —. W +	
	5. *Summer-(double) time		
	6. G.M.T.	*a.m., p.m.	21 14 00
	7. G.M.T. date		14 NOV. 1948

			H M S
STAGE 2	8. Sidereal Time noon G.M.T.		15 33 58
	9. Interval *TO or FROM noon	*p.m. +a.m. —	09 14 00 +
	Result		24 47 58
	10. Acceleration on interval	*p.m. + a.m.	01 31 +
	11. Sidereal Time at Greenwich at birth		24 49 29
	12. Longitude equivalent		0 32 —
	Long. × 4 = result in minutes	*E. I. W	
	13. LOCAL SIDEREAL TIME AT BIRTH		24 48 57
	Subtract 24 hours if necessary		24 00 00
STAGE 3	14. From Tables of Houses for Lat. 51° N 32'		48 57
	Asc 5 ♍ 12		
	M.C. 13·8·00		

FOR Lat. .... S. add 12 hours
Reverse signs
Asc. ....   M.C. ....

*Strike out whichever is not required.

Fig. A1.1

CALCULATION OF ZODIACAL POSITIONS OF PLANETS FOR GIVEN TIME

1. Enter birth date and time as given.
2. **CONVERT TO G.M.T.** by adding or subtracting Zone Standard. E −, W +.
3. If standard is G.M.T., state as o hours.
   If summer time, subtract 1 hour ; if double summer time, subtract 2 hours.
4. **Result is G.M.T.**
5. If result has altered date, enter.
6. Enter hours and minutes TO or FROM noon G.M.T. (before or after).
7. Fill in remainder of form as indicated.

STAGE 4

		D	M	Y
Birth date		14	NOV	1948

		h	m	s	
Birth time as given		21	14	00	a.m., ~~p.m.~~*
Zone Standard	*E −. W +				
*Summer– (double–) time					
G.M.T.		21	14	00	a.m., ~~p.m.~~*
G.M.T. date		14	NOV	1948	
Interval TO or FROM noon		9	14		
Log. of interval		4149			

PLANET	⊙	☽	☿	♀	♂	Moon's Dec.
Daily Motion	1.00	12.27	31	♄ 12	45	
Log. of Motion	1.3802	2850	1.6670	1300	1.5051	
Log. of interval	4149	4149	4149	4149	4149	
Addition of logs.	1.7951	6999	2.0819	1.7159	1.9200	

	⊙	☽	☿	♀	♂	N. S.*
Sign containing planet						
MIDNIGHT Noon position of planet	22 03	25 40	6 23	15 56	20 40	
Anti-log. of addition, a.m. −, p.m.+* (Reverse if retrograde)	23	4 48	12	28	17·1	
Position at given time	22 ♏ 26	00 ♉ 28	6 ♏ 35	16 ♈ 24	20 ♐ 57	

Fig. A1.1

Calculate the difference between noon or midnight and the birthtime GMT (Interval).

A conversion is needed to adjust mean time into sidereal time, called the acceleration on the interval. Correct the Sidereal Time using the formula: 10 seconds for each hour of Interval Time. Add or subtract depending on whether the birth is a.m. or p.m. and depending on which tables, Noon or Midnight, are being used.

Correct the Sidereal time for Longitude difference between Greenwich and birthplace using the formula: multiply by four the degree and minutes of longitude of the birthplace, and call the result minutes and seconds of time. If birthplace is East of Greenwich add the longitude equivalent, if West subtract.

The result is the Local Sidereal Time (LST) at birth.

Worked Example: Refer to Ephemeris Fig. A1.2 for Noon on the 14 November 1948 where the sidereal time is 15 hrs 33' 58". Irsert into Fig. A1.1, Interval from Noon to given birthtime of 21.14 is 9 hrs. 14 mins. Acceleration on Interval (10 secs for every hour) = 1 min. 30 secs. Longitude of birthplace is 00 °W 08 x 4 = result in minutes and seconds, 32 secs. Subtract 24 hours if necessary whenever the 'hour' column exceeds 24, since sidereal time reaches 24 hours and then starts from 0 hours, to keep a result between 0 and 24 hours. Result is the LST 00 hrs. 48 mins. 57 secs.

(For births in Southern latitudes, since any point in the Northern latitudes is separated from its opposite point in the Southern latitudes by 12 hours an addition of 12 hours is made to the LST. When the nearest sidereal time has been located in the Table of Houses (stage 3) the corresponding sign of both Ascendant and Midheaven is *reversed*. For example, if Prince Charles had been born in a Southern Latitude his Ascendant would be 5° Aquarius 12' the opposite sign to Leo. The signs in which the planets are placed (Stage 4) are NOT reversed.)

Stage 3: Calculating the Ascendant and Midheaven Positions

When the sidereal clock (star time) at London reads 0 hrs. 0 mins. 0 secs. then 0° Aries, the beginning degree of the zodiac, will lie due South on the Midheaven or 10th House cusp. A few minutes later these positions will change, hence the importance of the birthtime in determining the sign and degree that is on the Midheaven and Ascendant of the horoscope.

NOVEMBER 1948

DAY	EPHEMERIS SIDEREAL TIME	☉	☊	☽	☿	♀	♂	♃	♄	♅	♆	♇
	h m s	° ′	° ′	° ′	° ′	° ′	° ′	° ′	° ′	° ′	° ′	° ′
LONGITUDE at NOON												
1 T	14 42 43.2	8♏59.1	4♉38.5	12♏16.8	20♎52.2	0♎16.4	11♐ 3.4	27♐15.6	4♍22.4	0♋17.1	13♎41.9	16♌30.2
2 W	14 46 39.7	9 59.2	4 35.3	26 24.8	21 32.6	1 28.0	11 47.4	27 26.9	4 26.9	0R15.7	13 43.9	16 30.6
3 T	14 50 36.3	10 59.3	4 32.1	10♐12.4	22 21.0	2 39.8	12 31.5	27 38.3	4 31.4	0 14.4	13 46.0	16 31.0
4 F	14 54 32.8	11 59.5	4 29.0	23 37.2	23 16.4	3 51.7	13 15.6	27 49.8	4 35.8	0 12.9	13 48.0	16 31.4
5 S	14 58 29.4	12 59.7	4 25.8	6♑39.0	24 18.0	5 3.7	13 59.8	28 1.4	4 40.1	0 11.4	13 50.0	16 31.8
6 S	15 2 25.9	13 59.9	4 22.6	19 19.4	25 25.1	6 15.8	14 44.0	28 13.0	4 44.4	0 9.9	13 52.0	16 32.1
7 M	15 6 22.5	15 0.1	4 19.4	1♒41.2	26 36.9	7 27.9	15 28.4	28 24.7	4 48.5	0 8.3	13 54.0	16 32.4
8 T	15 10 19.1	16 0.4	4 16.3	13 48.4	27 52.7	8 40.2	16 12.7	28 36.5	4 52.5	0 6.7	13 55.9	16 32.7
9 W	15 14 15.6	17 0.7	4 13.1	25 45.6	29 12.0	9 52.6	16 57.2	28 48.4	4 56.5	0 5.1	13 57.9	16 32.9
10 T	15 18 12.2	18 1.0	4 9.9	7♓37.3	0♏34.1	11 5.0	17 41.7	29 0.3	5 0.4	0 3.4	13 59.8	16 33.1
11 F	15 22 8.7	19 1.4	4 6.7	19 28.5	1 58.7	12 17.5	18 26.2	29 12.4	5 4.1	0 1.7	14 1.7	16 33.3
12 S	15 26 5.3	20 1.7	4 3.5	1♈23.4	3 25.3	13 30.1	19 10.9	29 24.4	5 7.8	29♊59.9	14 3.6	16 33.5
13 S	15 30 1.8	21 2.1	4 0.4	13 26.1	4 53.6	14 42.8	19 55.6	29 36.6	5 11.4	29 58.1	14 5.5	16 33.6
14 M	15 33 58.4	22 2.5	3 57.2	25 39.9	6 23.3	15 55.6	20 40.3	29 48.8	5 14.9	29 56.3	14 7.4	16 33.7
15 T	15 37 55.0	23 3.0	3 54.0	8♉ 7.1	7 54.2	17 8.4	21 25.1	0♑ 1.1	5 18.3	29 54.4	14 9.2	16 33.8
16 W	15 41 51.5	24 3.4	3 50.8	20 49.3	9 25.9	18 21.4	22 10.0	0 13.5	5 21.6	29 52.5	14 11.0	16 33.8
17 T	15 45 48.0	25 3.9	3 47.7	3♊47.2	10 58.4	19 34.4	22 54.9	0 25.9	5 24.8	29 50.5	14 12.8	16 33.8
18 F	15 49 44.6	26 4.4	3 44.5	17 0.2	12 31.5	20 47.5	23 39.8	0 38.4	5 27.9	29 48.5	14 14.6	16R33.8
19 S	15 53 41.2	27 5.0	3 41.3	0♋27.4	14 5.0	22 0.6	24 24.9	0 51.0	5 30.9	29 46.5	14 16.4	16 33.8
20 S	15 57 37.7	28 5.6	3 38.1	14 6.9	15 38.8	23 13.8	25 10.0	1 3.6	5 33.8	29 44.4	14 18.1	16 33.7
21 M	16 1 34.3	29 6.2	3 35.0	27 56.7	17 12.9	24 27.1	25 55.1	1 16.3	5 36.7	29 42.3	14 19.8	16 33.6
22 T	16 5 30.8	0♐ 6.8	3 31.8	11♌54.9	18 47.2	25 40.5	26 40.3	1 29.0	5 39.4	29 40.2	14 21.5	16 33.5
23 W	16 9 27.4	1 7.4	3 28.6	25 59.4	20 21.6	26 53.9	27 25.6	1 41.8	5 42.0	29 38.1	14 23.2	16 33.3
24 T	16 13 23.0	2 8.1	3 25.4	10♍ 8.5	21 56.1	28 7.4	28 10.9	1 54.6	5 44.5	29 35.9	14 24.9	16 33.2
25 F	16 17 20.5	3 8.8	3 22.3	24 20.4	23 30.6	29 21.0	28 56.3	2 7.5	5 46.9	29 33.7	14 26.5	16 33.0
26 S	16 21 17.1	4 9.6	3 19.1	8♎33.3	25 5.1	0♏34.6	29 41.7	2 20.5	5 49.2	29 31.5	14 28.1	16 32.7
27 S	16 25 13.6	5 10.3	3 15.9	22 44.6	26 39.6	1 48.3	0♑27.2	2 33.5	5 51.4	29 29.2	14 29.7	16 32.5
28 M	16 29 10.2	6 11.1	3 12.7	6♏51.6	28 14.1	3 2.1	1 12.8	2 46.6	5 53.5	29 26.9	14 31.2	16 32.2
29 T	16 33 6.8	7 12.0	3 9.6	20 50.9	29 48.5	4 15.8	1 58.4	2 59.7	5 55.4	29 24.6	14 32.7	16 31.8
30 W	16 37 3.3	8 12.8	3 6.4	4♐39.1	1♐22.9	5 29.7	2 44.0	3 12.8	5 57.3	29 22.3	14 34.2	16 31.5
DECLINATION at NOON												
1 T	14 42 43.2	14S29.8	13N 4.4	16S10.3	6S17.8	1N16.0	22S56.3	23S19.6	11N12.3	23N38.6	4S 0.5	23N 1.8
4 F	14 54 32.8	15 26.4	13 1.2	27 15.7	6 60.0	0S 4.2	23 15.1	23 20.6	11 8.0	23 38.7	4 2.8	23 2.2
7 M	15 6 22.5	16 20.6	12 58.0	24 55.6	8 11.8	1 25.2	23 31.9	23 21.4	11 3.9	23 38.7	4 5.0	23 2.7
10 T	15 18 12.2	17 12.3	12 54.7	12 50.0	9 42.1	2 46.6	23 46.5	23 22.1	11 0.2	23 38.8	4 7.2	23 3.3
13 S	15 30 1.8	18 1.4	12 51.5	3N31.2	11 22.1	4 8.2	23 58.9	23 22.6	10 56.7	23 38.8	4 9.3	23 4.0
16 W	15 41 51.5	18 47.6	12 48.3	19 21.3	13 5.7	5 29.5	24 9.1	23 22.9	10 53.6	23 38.9	4 11.3	23 4.7
19 S	15 53 41.2	19 30.8	12 45.1	27 46.4	14 48.8	6 50.3	24 17.1	23 23.1	10 50.8	23 38.9	4 13.3	23 5.5
22 T	16 5 30.8	20 10.9	12 41.8	22 12.1	16 28.4	8 10.1	24 22.6	23 23.0	10 48.4	23 39.0	4 15.2	23 6.4
25 F	16 17 20.5	20 47.6	12 38.6	5 21.7	18 2.5	9 28.8	24 25.9	23 22.8	10 46.2	23 39.0	4 17.0	23 7.4
28 M	16 29 10.2	21 20.9	12 35.3	13S59.6	19 29.7	10 45.9	24 26.7	23 22.4	10 44.5	23 39.0	4 18.7	23 8.4

DECEMBER 1948

DAY	EPHEMERIS SIDEREAL TIME	☉	☊	☽	☿	♀	♂	♃	♄	♅	♆	♇
LONGITUDE at NOON												
1 T	16 40 59.8	9♐13.6	3♉ 3.2	18♐12.8	2♐57.2	6♏43.6	3♑29.7	3♑26.0	5♍59.1	29♊19.9	14♎35.7	16♌31.1
2 F	16 44 56.4	10 14.5	3 0.0	1♑29.4	4 31.5	7 57.5	4 15.5	3 39.2	6 0.7	29R17.5	14 37.2	16R30.7
3 S	16 48 53.0	11 15.4	2 56.8	14 27.6	6 5.7	9 11.5	5 1.3	3 52.5	6 2.3	29 15.1	14 38.6	16 30.3
4 S	16 52 49.6	12 16.3	2 53.7	27 7.2	7 39.9	10 25.5	5 47.1	4 5.9	6 3.7	29 12.7	14 40.0	16 29.8
5 M	16 56 46.1	13 17.3	2 50.5	9♒29.8	9 14.1	11 39.6	6 33.0	4 19.2	6 5.0	29 10.3	14 41.3	16 29.3
6 T	17 0 42.6	14 18.2	2 47.3	21 37.9	10 48.3	12 53.7	7 19.0	4 32.6	6 6.2	29 7.8	14 42.7	16 28.8
7 W	17 4 39.2	15 19.1	2 44.1	3♓35.3	12 22.4	14 7.8	8 5.0	4 46.1	6 7.3	29 5.3	14 44.0	16 28.3
8 T	17 8 35.8	16 20.1	2 41.0	15 26.5	13 56.6	15 22.0	8 51.0	4 59.5	6 8.3	29 2.8	14 45.3	16 27.7
9 F	17 12 32.3	17 21.1	2 37.8	27 16.7	15 30.8	16 36.2	9 37.1	5 13.0	6 9.2	29 0.3	14 46.5	16 27.1
10 S	17 16 28.9	18 22.1	2 34.6	9♈11.1	17 5.0	17 50.5	10 23.2	5 26.6	6 10.0	28 57.8	14 47.8	16 26.5
11 S	17 20 25.4	19 23.0	2 31.4	21 14.7	18 39.3	19 4.7	11 9.4	5 40.1	6 10.7	28 55.3	14 49.0	16 25.9
12 M	17 24 22.0	20 24.1	2 28.3	3♉32.1	20 13.6	20 19.1	11 55.6	5 53.7	6 11.2	28 52.8	14 50.1	16 25.2
13 T	17 28 18.5	21 25.1	2 25.1	16 7.3	21 48.1	21 33.4	12 41.9	6 7.3	6 11.6	28 50.2	14 51.3	16 24.5
14 W	17 32 15.1	22 26.1	2 21.9	29 2.8	23 22.6	22 47.8	13 28.2	6 21.0	6 12.0	28 47.7	14 52.4	16 23.8
15 T	17 36 11.7	23 27.1	2 18.7	12♊19.8	24 57.2	24 2.2	14 14.5	6 34.7	6 12.2	28 45.1	14 53.4	16 23.1
16 F	17 40 8.2	24 28.2	2 15.6	25 57.3	26 32.0	25 16.7	15 0.9	6 48.4	6 12.3	28 42.6	14 54.5	16 22.3
17 S	17 44 4.8	25 29.2	2 12.4	9♋52.6	28 6.9	26 31.1	15 47.3	7 2.1	6R12.3	28 40.0	14 55.5	16 21.5
18 S	17 48 1.3	26 30.3	2 9.2	24 1.5	29 42.0	27 45.6	16 33.8	7 15.8	6 12.2	28 37.4	14 56.5	16 20.7
19 M	17 51 57.9	27 31.4	2 6.0	8♌18.7	1♑17.2	29 0.2	17 20.3	7 29.6	6 11.9	28 34.8	14 57.4	16 19.9
20 T	17 55 54.5	28 32.4	2 2.8	22 38.8	2 52.6	0♐14.7	18 6.8	7 43.4	6 11.6	28 32.3	14 58.3	16 19.0
21 W	17 59 51.0	29 33.5	1 59.7	6♍57.2	4 28.2	1 29.3	18 53.4	7 57.2	6 11.1	28 29.7	14 59.2	16 18.1
22 T	18 3 47.6	0♑34.7	1 56.5	21 10.6	6 4.0	2 44.0	19 40.0	8 11.0	6 10.6	28 27.1	15 0.1	16 17.2
23 F	18 7 44.2	1 35.8	1 53.3	5♎16.7	7 40.0	3 58.6	20 26.7	8 24.8	6 9.9	28 24.5	15 0.9	16 16.3
24 S	18 11 40.7	2 36.9	1 50.1	19 14.6	9 16.1	5 13.3	21 13.4	8 38.7	6 9.1	28 22.0	15 1.7	16 15.4
25 S	18 15 37.2	3 38.1	1 47.0	3♏ 4.2	10 52.5	6 28.0	22 0.1	8 52.5	6 8.2	28 19.4	15 2.5	16 14.4
26 M	18 19 33.8	4 39.2	1 43.8	16 45.2	12 29.1	7 42.7	22 46.9	9 6.4	6 7.2	28 16.8	15 3.2	16 13.4
27 T	18 23 30.4	5 40.4	1 40.6	0♐17.3	14 5.8	8 57.5	23 33.7	9 20.3	6 6.1	28 14.3	15 3.9	16 12.4
28 W	18 27 26.9	6 41.6	1 37.4	13 39.7	15 42.7	10 12.2	24 20.5	9 34.2	6 4.9	28 11.8	15 4.5	16 11.4
29 T	18 31 23.5	7 42.8	1 34.3	26 51.1	17 19.7	11 27.0	25 7.4	9 48.1	6 3.5	28 9.2	15 5.2	16 10.3
30 F	18 35 20.0	8 43.9	1 31.1	9♑50.2	18 56.7	12 41.8	25 54.3	10 2.0	6 2.1	28 6.7	15 5.8	16 9.3
31 S	18 39 16.6	9 45.1	1 27.9	22 35.8	20 33.9	13 56.6	26 41.2	10 15.9	6 0.6	28 4.2	15 6.3	16 8.2
DECLINATION at NOON												
1 T	16 40 59.8	21S50.5	12N32.1	26S29.5	20S48.8	12S 1.0	24S25.0	23S21.8	10N43.1	23N39.0	4S20.3	23N 9.5
4 S	16 52 49.6	22 16.4	12 28.8	25 46.2	21 59.1	13 13.8	24 20.9	23 20.9	10 42.0	23 39.0	4 21.8	23 10.7
7 W	17 4 39.2	22 38.4	12 25.6	14 23.3	22 59.6	14 23.9	24 14.4	23 19.9	10 41.4	23 39.0	4 23.2	23 12.0
10 S	17 16 28.9	22 56.3	12 22.3	1N38.2	23 49.8	15 31.0	24 5.4	23 18.6	10 41.1	23 39.0	4 24.5	23 13.3
13 T	17 28 18.5	23 10.2	12 19.0	17 41.8	24 29.0	16 34.7	23 53.9	23 17.1	10 41.1	23 39.0	4 25.7	23 14.6
16 F	17 40 8.2	23 19.9	12 15.7	27 25.0	24 56.5	17 34.6	23 39.9	23 15.4	10 41.6	23 38.9	4 26.8	23 16.0
19 M	17 51 57.9	23 25.5	12 12.5	23 5.2	25 11.8	18 30.5	23 23.6	23 13.5	10 42.4	23 38.9	4 27.8	23 17.5
22 T	18 3 47.6	23 26.8	12 9.2	6 38.4	25 14.3	19 22.0	23 4.8	23 11.3	10 43.6	23 38.8	4 28.7	23 19.0
25 S	18 15 37.2	23 23.9	12 5.9	12S31.8	25 3.6	20 8.7	22 43.6	23 8.9	10 45.1	23 38.7	4 29.4	23 20.5
28 W	18 27 26.9	23 16.7	12 2.6	25 43.3	24 39.1	20 50.4	22 20.1	23 6.3	10 47.0	23 38.7	4 30.1	23 22.1
31 S	18 39 16.6	23 5.4	11 59.3	26 26.3	24 0.7	21 26.7	21 54.3	23 3.5	10 49.3	23 38.6	4 30.6	23 23.6

Fig. A1.2

To find the given Ascendant and Midheaven positions, refer to the Table of Houses and locate the nearest sidereal time to the local sidereal time arrived at in Stage 2. The numbers at the top of each column are the numbers of the houses of the chart, 10th, 11th, 12th, Ascendant, 2nd, 3rd using the Placidean House System. For beginners it is recommended to use Equal House so we only want to know the sign and degree for the Midheaven and Ascendant. Having determined the Ascendant each House contains exactly 30°. (Additional calculations may be done to arrive at a precise Ascendant degree and minutes position but the computation given here is sufficient for beginners.)

Having determined the Ascendant position this can now be inserted on the blank chart form.

Worked Example: Prince Charles' LST is 00 hrs. 48 mins. 57 secs. which on Table A1.3 reads Ascendant 5° Leo 12', Midheaven 13° Aries 00'. Using Equal House system the House cusps can now be plotted, Fig. A2.1. On the left hand side (at the 9 o'clock position, the eastern horizon) can be seen the Ascendant at 5° Leo 12'. Near the top of the chart an arrow indicates the Midheaven position at 13° Aries. The Ascendant is the First House cusp and the figure 5° 12' will be on each house cusp. The sign and degree of the Ascendant is inserted first and the rest of the signs follow on in their correct order FROM the Ascendant (i.e. anti-clockwise).

Stage 4: Calculating the Planetary Positions

Having established the time of birth in sidereal time and in relation to the birthplace the actual planetary positions need to be determined. The planetary positions are listed in the Ephemeris as at Noon or Midnight. If your time of birth is later than Noon then these positions will have moved along slightly on the ecliptic path, if before Noon the actual positions will be a little earlier along the ecliptic path. To be exact, we have to apply this difference to arrive at its position at the moment of birth.

The first step is to determine how far each planet travels in a 24 hour period – its Daily Motion. This is done using scrap paper, taking the Noon or Midnight position on the day of birth and the Noon or Midnight position of the following or previous day (dependent upon which Tables you are using). The Log of the Daily Motion is added to the Log of the Interval and the Anti-Log of this will give the actual distance travelled by the planet from Noon or Midnight To or From the actual time of birth. These calculations are done for the Daily Motion of the Sun, Moon and

PROPORTIONAL LOGARITHMS FOR FINDING THE PLANETS' PLACES
DEGREES OR HOURS

Min.	0	1	2	3	4	5	6	7	8	9	10	11	12	13	14	15	Min.
0	3.1584	1.3802	1.0792	9031	7781	6812	6021	5351	4771	4260	3802	3388	3010	2663	2341	2041	0
1	3.1584	1.3730	1.0756	9007	7763	6798	6009	5341	4762	4252	3795	3382	3004	2657	2336	2036	1
2	2.8573	1.3660	1.0720	8983	7745	6784	5997	5330	4753	4244	3788	3375	2998	2652	2330	2032	2
3	2.6812	1.3590	1.0685	8959	7728	6769	5985	5320	4744	4236	3780	3368	2992	2646	2325	2027	3
4	2.5563	1.3522	1.0649	8935	7710	6755	5973	5310	4735	4228	3773	3362	2986	2640	2320	2022	4
5	2.4594	1.3454	1.0614	8912	7692	6741	5961	5300	4726	4220	3766	3355	2980	2635	2315	2017	5
6	2.3802	1.3388	1.0580	8888	7674	6726	5949	5289	4717	4212	3759	3349	2974	2629	2310	2012	6
7	2.3133	1.3323	1.0546	8865	7657	6712	5937	5279	4708	4204	3752	3342	2968	2624	2305	2008	7
8	2.2553	1.3258	1.0511	8842	7639	6698	5925	5269	4699	4196	3745	3336	2962	2618	2300	2003	8
9	2.2041	1.3195	1.0478	8819	7622	6684	5913	5259	4690	4188	3737	3329	2956	2613	2295	1998	9
10	2.1584	1.3133	1.0444	8796	7604	6670	5902	5249	4682	4180	3730	3323	2950	2607	2289	1993	10
11	2.1170	1.3071	1.0411	8773	7587	6656	5890	5239	4673	4172	3723	3316	2944	2602	2284	1988	11
12	2.0792	1.3010	1.0378	8751	7570	6642	5878	5229	4664	4164	3716	3310	2938	2596	2279	1984	12
13	2.0444	1.2950	1.0345	8728	7552	6628	5866	5219	4655	4156	3709	3303	2933	2591	2274	1979	13
14	2.0122	1.2891	1.0313	8706	7535	6614	5855	5209	4646	4148	3702	3297	2927	2585	2269	1974	14
15	1.9823	1.2833	1.0280	8683	7518	6600	5843	5199	4638	4141	3695	3291	2921	2580	2264	1969	15
16	1.9542	1.2775	1.0248	8661	7501	6587	5832	5189	4629	4133	3688	3284	2915	2574	2259	1965	16
17	1.9279	1.2719	1.0216	8639	7484	6573	5820	5179	4620	4125	3681	3278	2909	2569	2254	1960	17
18	1.9031	1.2663	1.0185	8617	7467	6559	5809	5169	4611	4117	3674	3271	2903	2564	2249	1955	18
19	1.8796	1.2607	1.0153	8595	7451	6546	5797	5159	4603	4109	3667	3265	2897	2558	2244	1950	19
20	1.8573	1.2553	1.0122	8573	7434	6532	5786	5149	4594	4102	3660	3258	2891	2553	2239	1946	20
21	1.8361	1.2499	1.0091	8552	7417	6519	5774	5139	4585	4094	3653	3252	2885	2547	2234	1941	21
22	1.8159	1.2445	1.0061	8530	7401	6505	5763	5129	4577	4086	3646	3246	2880	2542	2229	1936	22
23	1.7966	1.2393	1.0030	8509	7384	6492	5752	5120	4568	4079	3639	3239	2874	2536	2223	1932	23
24	1.7781	1.2341	1.0000	8487	7368	6478	5740	5110	4559	4071	3632	3233	2868	2531	2218	1927	24
25	1.7604	1.2289	0.9970	8466	7351	6465	5729	5100	4551	4063	3625	3227	2862	2526	2213	1922	25
26	1.7434	1.2239	0.9940	8445	7335	6451	5718	5090	4542	4055	3618	3220	2856	2520	2208	1917	26
27	1.7270	1.2188	0.9910	8424	7318	6438	5706	5081	4534	4048	3611	3214	2850	2515	2203	1913	27
28	1.7112	1.2139	0.9881	8403	7302	6425	5695	5071	4525	4040	3604	3208	2845	2509	2198	1908	28
29	1.6960	1.2090	0.9852	8382	7286	6412	5684	5061	4516	4032	3597	3201	2839	2504	2193	1903	29
30	1.6812	1.2041	0.9823	8361	7270	6398	5673	5051	4508	4025	3590	3195	2833	2499	2188	1899	30
31	1.6670	1.1993	0.9794	8341	7254	6385	5662	5042	4499	4017	3583	3189	2827	2493	2183	1894	31
32	1.6532	1.1946	0.9765	8320	7238	6372	5651	5032	4491	4010	3576	3183	2821	2488	2178	1889	32
33	1.6398	1.1899	0.9737	8300	7222	6359	5640	5023	4482	4002	3570	3176	2816	2483	2173	1885	33
34	1.6269	1.1852	0.9708	8279	7206	6346	5629	5013	4474	3994	3563	3170	2810	2477	2168	1880	34
35	1.6143	1.1806	0.9680	8259	7190	6333	5618	5003	4466	3987	3556	3164	2804	2472	2164	1875	35
36	1.6021	1.1761	0.9652	8239	7174	6320	5607	4994	4457	3979	3549	3157	2798	2467	2159	1871	36
37	1.5902	1.1716	0.9625	8219	7159	6307	5596	4984	4449	3972	3542	3151	2793	2461	2154	1866	37
38	1.5786	1.1671	0.9597	8199	7143	6294	5585	4975	4440	3964	3535	3145	2787	2456	2149	1862	38
39	1.5673	1.1627	0.9570	8179	7128	6282	5574	4965	4432	3957	3529	3139	2781	2451	2144	1857	39
40	1.5563	1.1584	0.9542	8159	7112	6269	5563	4956	4424	3949	3522	3133	2775	2445	2139	1852	40
41	1.5456	1.1540	0.9515	8140	7097	6256	5552	4947	4415	3942	3515	3126	2770	2440	2134	1848	41
42	1.5351	1.1498	0.9488	8120	7081	6243	5541	4937	4407	3934	3508	3120	2764	2435	2129	1843	42
43	1.5249	1.1455	0.9462	8101	7066	6231	5531	4928	4399	3927	3501	3114	2758	2430	2124	1838	43
44	1.5149	1.1413	0.9435	8081	7050	6218	5520	4918	4390	3919	3495	3108	2753	2424	2119	1834	44
45	1.5051	1.1372	0.9409	8062	7035	6205	5509	4909	4382	3912	3488	3102	2747	2419	2114	1829	45
46	1.4956	1.1331	0.9383	8043	7020	6193	5498	4900	4374	3905	3481	3096	2741	2414	2109	1825	46
47	1.4863	1.1290	0.9356	8023	7005	6180	5488	4890	4365	3897	3475	3089	2736	2409	2104	1820	47
48	1.4771	1.1249	0.9330	8004	6990	6168	5477	4881	4357	3890	3468	3083	2730	2403	2099	1816	48
49	1.4682	1.1209	0.9305	7985	6875	6155	5466	4872	4349	3882	3461	3077	2724	2398	2095	1811	49
50	1.4594	1.1170	0.9279	7966	6960	6143	5456	4863	4341	3875	3454	3071	2719	2393	2090	1806	50
51	1.4508	1.1130	0.9254	7947	6945	6131	5445	4853	4333	3868	3448	3065	2713	2388	2085	1802	51
52	1.4424	1.1091	0.9228	7929	6930	6118	5434	4844	4324	3860	3441	3059	2707	2382	2080	1797	52
53	1.4341	1.1053	0.9203	7910	6915	6106	5424	4835	4316	3853	3434	3053	2702	2377	2075	1793	53
54	1.4260	1.1015	0.9178	7891	6900	6094	5414	4826	4308	3846	3428	3047	2696	2372	2070	1788	54
55	1.4180	1.0977	0.9153	7873	6885	6081	5403	4817	4300	3838	3421	3041	2691	2367	2065	1784	55
56	1.4102	1.0939	0.9128	7854	6871	6069	5393	4808	4292	3831	3415	3034	2685	2362	2061	1779	56
57	1.4025	1.0902	0.9104	7836	6856	6057	5382	4798	4284	3824	3408	3028	2679	2356	2056	1774	57
58	1.3949	1.0865	0.9079	7818	6841	6045	5372	4789	4276	3817	3401	3022	2674	2351	2051	1770	58
59	1.3875	1.0828	0.9055	7800	6827	6033	5361	4780	4268	3809	3395	3016	2668	2346	2046	1765	59
	0	1	2	3	4	5	6	7	8	9	10	11	12	13	14	15	

RULE:—Add proportional log. of planet's daily motion to log. of time from noon, and the sum will be the log. of the motion required. Add this to planet's place at noon, if time be p.m., but subtract if a.m. and the sum will be planet's true place. If Retrograde, subtract for p.m., but add for a.m.

What is the Long. of ☽ Apr. 1, 1993 at 2.15 p.m.?

☽'s daily motion—14° 12'	
Prop. Log. of 14° 12'	.2279
Prop. Log. of 2h. 15m.	1.0280
☽'s motion in 2h. 15m. = 1° 20' or Log.	1.2559

☽'s Long. = 28° ♋ 38' + 1° 20' = 29° ♋ 58'
The Daily Motions of the Sun, Moon, Mercury, Venus and Mars will be found on pages 26 to 28.

Fig. A1.3

TABLES OF HOUSES FOR LONDON, Latitude 51° 32' N.

Sidereal Time (H. M. S.)	10 ♈	11 ♉	12 ♊	Ascen ♋ (° ')	2 ♌	3 ♍
0 0 0	0	9	22	26	26 36	12	3
0 3 40	1	10	23	27	17 13	3
0 7 20	2	11	24	27	50 14	4
0 11 0	3	12	25	28	42 15	5
0 14 41	4	13	25	29	17 15	6
0 18 21	5	14	26	29	55 16	7
0 22 2	6	15	27	0♌	34 17	8
0 25 42	7	16	28	1	14 18	8
0 29 23	8	17	29	1	55 18	9
0 33 4	9	18	♋	2	33 19	10
0 36 45	10	19	1	3	14 20	11
0 40 26	11	20	1	3	54 20	12
0 44 8	12	21	2	4	33 21	13
0 47 50	13	22	3	5	12 22	14
0 51 32	14	23	4	5	52 23	15
0 55 14	15	24	5	6	30 23	15
0 58 57	16	25	6	7	9 24	16
1 2 40	17	26	6	7	50 25	17
1 6 23	18	27	7	8	30 26	18
1 10 7	19	28	8	9	26 26	19
1 13 51	20	29	9	9	48 27	19
1 17 35	21	♊	10	10	28 28	20
1 21 20	22	1	10	11	8 28	21
1 25 6	23	2	11	11	48 29	22
1 28 52	24	3	12	12	28 ♍	23
1 32 38	25	4	13	13	8 1	24
1 36 25	26	4	14	13	48 1	25
1 40 12	27	6	14	14	28 2	25
1 44 0	28	7	15	15	8 3	26
1 47 48	29	8	16	15	48 4	27
1 51 37	30	9	17	16	28 4	28

Sidereal Time (H. M. S.)	10 ♉	11 ♊	12 ♋	Ascen ♌ (° ')	2 ♍	3 ♍
1 51 37	0	9	17	16	28 4	28
1 55 27	1	10	18	17	8 5	29
1 59 17	2	11	19	17	48 6	♎
2 3 8	3	12	19	18	28 7	1
2 6 59	4	13	20	19	9 8	2
2 10 51	5	14	21	19	40 9	2
2 14 44	6	15	22	20	29 9	3
2 18 37	7	16	22	21	10 10	4
2 22 31	8	17	23	21	51 11	5
2 26 25	9	18	24	22	32 11	6
2 30 20	10	19	25	23	14 12	7
2 34 16	11	20	25	23	55 13	8
2 38 13	12	21	26	24	36 14	9
2 42 10	13	22	27	25	17 15	10
2 46 8	14	23	28	25	58 15	11
2 50 7	15	24	29	26	40 16	12
2 54 7	16	25	29	27	22 17	12
2 58 7	17	26	♌	28	4 18	13
3 2 8	18	27	1	28	46 18	14
3 6 9	19	27	2	29	28 19	15
3 10 12	20	28	3	0♍	10 20	16
3 14 15	21	29	3	0	54 21	17
3 18 19	22	♋	4	1	36 22	18
3 22 23	23	1	5	2	20 22	19
3 26 29	24	2	6	3	2 23	20
3 30 35	25	3	7	3	45 24	21
3 34 41	26	4	7	4	28 25	22
3 38 49	27	5	8	5	11 26	23
3 42 57	28	6	9	5	54 27	24
3 47 6	29	7	10	6	38 27	25
3 51 15	30	8	11	7	21 28	25

Sidereal Time (H. M. S.)	10 ♊	11 ♋	12 ♌	Ascen ♍ (° ')	2 ♍	3 ♎
3 51 15	0	8	11	7	21 28	25
3 55 25	1	9	12	8	9 29	26
3 59 36	2	10	12	8	49 ♎	27
4 3 48	3	10	13	9	33 1	28
4 8 0	4	11	14	10	17 2	29
4 12 13	5	12	15	11	2 2	♏
4 16 26	6	13	16	11	46 3	1
4 20 40	7	14	17	12	30 4	2
4 24 55	8	15	17	13	15 5	3
4 29 10	9	16	18	14	0 6	4
4 33 26	10	17	19	14	45 7	5
4 37 42	11	18	20	15	30 8	6
4 41 59	12	19	21	16	15 8	7
4 46 16	13	20	21	17	0 9	8
4 50 34	14	21	22	17	45 10	9
4 54 52	15	22	23	18	30 11	10
4 59 10	16	23	24	19	16 12	11
5 3 29	17	24	25	20	3 13	12
5 7 49	18	25	26	20	49 14	13
5 12 9	19	25	27	21	35 14	14
5 16 29	20	26	28	22	20 15	14
5 20 49	21	27	28	23	6 16	15
5 25 9	22	28	29	23	51 17	16
5 29 30	23	29	♏	24	37 18	17
5 33 51	24	♌	1	25	23 19	18
5 38 12	25	1	2	26	9 20	19
5 42 34	26	2	3	26	55 21	20
5 46 55	27	3	4	27	41 21	21
5 51 17	28	4	4	28	27 22	22
5 55 38	29	5	5	29	13 23	23
6 0 0	30	6	6	30	0 24	24

Sidereal Time (H. M. S.)	10 ♋	11 ♌	12 ♍	Ascen ♎ (° ')	2	3 ♏
6 0 0	0	6	6	0	0 24	24
6 4 22	1	7	7	0	47 25	25
6 8 43	2	8	8	1	33 26	26
6 13 5	3	9	9	2	19 27	27
6 17 26	4	10	10	3	5 27	28
6 21 48	5	11	10	3	51 28	29
6 26 9	6	12	11	4	37 29	♐
6 30 30	7	13	12	5	23 ♏	1
6 34 51	8	14	13	6	9 1	2
6 39 11	9	15	14	6	55 2	3
6 43 31	10	16	16	7	40 2	4
6 47 51	11	16	16	8	26 3	4
6 52 11	12	17	17	9	12 4	5
6 56 31	13	18	17	9	58 5	6
7 0 50	14	19	18	10	43 6	7
7 5 8	15	20	19	11	28 7	8
7 9 26	16	21	20	12	14 8	9
7 13 44	17	22	21	12	59 8	10
7 18 1	18	23	22	13	45 9	11
7 22 18	19	24	23	14	30 10	12
7 26 34	20	25	24	15	15 11	13
7 30 50	21	26	25	16	0 12	14
7 35 5	22	27	25	16	43 13	15
7 39 20	23	28	26	17	30 13	16
7 43 34	24	29	27	18	15 14	17
7 47 47	25	♍	28	18	57 15	18
7 52 0	26	1	29	19	43 16	19
7 56 12	27	2	29	20	27 17	20
8 0 24	28	3	♎	21	11 18	20
8 4 35	29	4	1	21	56 18	21
8 8 45	30	5	2	22	40 19	22

Sidereal Time (H. M. S.)	10 ♌	11 ♍	12 ♎	Ascen ♎ (° ')	2 ♏	3 ♐
8 8 45	0	5	2	22	40 19	22
8 12 54	1	5	3	23	24 20	23
8 17 3	2	6	3	24	7 21	24
8 21 11	3	7	4	24	50 22	25
8 25 19	4	8	5	25	34 23	26
8 29 26	5	9	6	26	18 23	27
8 33 31	6	10	7	27	1 24	28
8 37 37	7	11	8	27	44 25	29
8 41 41	8	12	8	28	26 26	♑
8 45 45	9	13	9	29	8 27	1
8 49 48	10	14	10	29	50 27	2
8 53 51	11	15	11	0♏	32 28	3
8 57 52	12	16	12	1	15 29	4
9 1 53	13	17	12	1	58 ♐	4
9 5 53	14	18	13	2	39 1	5
9 9 53	15	19	14	3	21 1	6
9 13 52	16	19	15	4	3 2	7
9 17 50	17	20	16	4	44 3	8
9 21 47	18	21	16	5	26 3	9
9 25 44	19	22	17	6	7 4	10
9 29 40	20	23	18	6	48 5	11
9 33 35	21	24	18	7	29 5	12
9 37 29	22	25	19	8	9 6	13
9 41 23	23	26	20	8	50 7	14
9 45 16	24	27	21	9	31 8	15
9 49 9	25	28	22	10	11 9	16
9 53 1	26	28	23	10	51 9	17
9 56 52	27	29	23	11	32 10	18
10 0 42	28	♎	24	12	11 11	19
10 4 33	29	1	25	12	53 12	20
10 8 23	30	2	26	13	33 13	20

Sidereal Time (H. M. S.)	10 ♍	11 ♎	12 ♎	Ascen ♏ (° ')	2 ♐	3 ♑
10 8 23	0	2	2	13	33 13	20
10 12 12	1	3	26	14	13 14	21
10 16 0	2	4	27	14	53 15	22
10 19 48	3	5	28	15	33 15	23
10 23 35	4	5	29	16	13 16	24
10 27 22	5	6	29	16	27 17	25
10 31 8	6	7	♏	17	32 18	26
10 34 54	7	8	1	18	12 19	27
10 38 40	8	9	2	18	52 20	28
10 42 25	9	10	2	19	31 20	29
10 46 9	10	11	3	20	11 21	♒
10 49 53	11	11	4	20	50 22	1
10 53 37	12	12	4	21	30 23	2
10 57 20	13	13	5	22	9 24	3
11 1 1	14	14	6	22	49 24	4
11 4 46	15	15	7	23	28 25	5
11 8 28	16	16	7	24	8 26	6
11 12 10	17	17	8	24	47 27	8
11 15 52	18	17	9	25	27 27	8
11 19 34	19	18	10	26	6 29	10
11 23 15	20	19	11	27	25 ♒	11
11 26 56	21	20	11	27	25 0	12
11 30 37	22	21	12	28	1 1	13
11 34 18	23	22	13	28	44 2	14
11 37 58	24	23	13	29	24 3	15
11 41 39	25	24	14	♐	3 4	16
11 45 19	26	24	15	0	43 5	17
11 49 0	27	25	15	1	23 6	18
11 52 40	28	26	16	2	3 6	19
11 56 20	29	27	17	2	43 7	20
12 0 0	30	27	17	3	13 8	21

Fig. A1.3

for the planets Mercury, Venus and Mars. A glance at the Ephemeris will show that the daily motion of planets Jupiter, Saturn, Uranus, Neptune and Pluto is very small and can be easily worked out in one's head.

Occasionally planets appear, as seen from the Earth, to be moving backwards to the normal direct movement, astrologically termed *retrograde*. When this happens (denoted by a small R in the Ephemeris column), the calculation of the planet's position is reversed.

Having listed the planetary positions by their longitude they can be written in the chart.

Worked Example: Prince Charles, The Sun position on 14 November 1948 Noon is 22 ° Scorpio 03' and on 15 November its position is 23 ° Scorpio 03'. In a period of 24 hours the Sun has moved 1 degree. The Log of the Daily Motion is 1.3804 and the Log of the Interval is 0.4149 which added together = 1.7951, the Anti-Log for which is 23 mins which, when added to the position at Noon on the 14 November 1948, gives the Sun position of 22 ° Scorpio 26'. (Refer Fig A 2.1)

Stage 4: Calculating the Planetary Aspects

The planetary positions can now be plotted on the horoscope wheel and the aspects, the angular relationship between planets and angles, defined. Where two planets are separated by a certain number of degrees (the aspect) this angular relationship is associated with significant effects. This is very evident to anyone through the Lunar phases – the Full and New Moon cycle, and its effect upon tidal flow. An aspect in a birth chart corresponds with an *accentuation* of the characteristics associated with the principles of those planets. The main aspects used in astrology are listed in Table A1.4.

An orb is allowed either side of exactitude for this effect. Refer to Table A1.4 where the aspects are listed and note the exact aspect distance and the 'allowed' orb of effect. A conjunction where the angular relationship is 0° can still be effective when the planets involved are up to 8° in distance. For example, if Venus is at 5° Aries and Mercury is at 13° Aries there exists a conjunction between Venus and Mercury of an allowable orb distance of 8°. Obviously the closer the aspect the greater its strength. For ease, the astrologer uses notation form for aspects as given in the table and used in the aspect grid on Fig. A2.1. Identifying aspects is frequently difficult for students but comes quickly with practice.

Table A1.4

Ang. separation	Orb	Name	Strength
0°	± 8°	conjunction	gives strength
30°	± 5°	sextile	ease
90°	± 8°	square	challenging
120°	± 5°	trine	ease
180°	± 8°	opposition	challenging

Worked Example: Prince Charles. The aspects have been worked out and are given in the aspect grid and drawn in to Chart of A 2.1.

Stage 5: Interpretation Of The Horoscope

Having computed the horoscope for a given time, date and place the next step is the interpretation and delineation. A full character assessment of Prince Charles is given in Appendix 2.

An Example Astrological Horoscope Interpretation

His Royal Highness Prince Charles

Throughout the history of astrology it has been a standard practice to examine and interpret the astrological portents of people who are in the Public Eye. In ancient times *only* the horoscopes of Kings, Queens, Rulers and Countries were of importance and any astrological indications carefully observed. It is widely accepted that long ago in Babylonian times astrologers tended to a high level of reported accuracy in interpretation, a factor which evades the modern professional who comes armed with computer programmes, tables, textbooks and journals to predict accurately and continually the unfolding wisdom of the heavens.

The emphasis upon individual astrological 'interpretation' became popular in the Victorian era both as a parlour game and as a fairground attraction. Present day astrology still carries these images despite efforts to bring a more professional approach and serious attitude.

Astrology today is generally used to counsel and advise. Modern day astrological textbooks focus on the rich, famous and infamous personalities, since whatever occurs in any dramatic manner will be recorded and timed; timing, of course, being of the essence in astrology.

The easiest astrology is retrospective prediction. It is easy to write text concerning events that have happened and to make the astrology 'fit the pattern' or simply to read into the symbolism that which is now so obvious. Making clear, concise and *precise* forthcoming predictions is much harder and few are willing to put pen to paper for fear of ridicule.

It should be clear that astrology is not about prediction but about guidance, counselling the individual to take greater control and to direct his life path in a more conscious manner. Specific events are less important than are given periods of time. It is very possible to predict, for example, that a marriage will become stressful, challenging and distressing over a period of, say, two years. That such will end in divorce is not as predictable and depends very much on the manner in which the parties deal with their problems, how they handle the difficulties. The astrologer can often predict the period when the seeds are sown for a marriage breakdown, and the individual knowing the consequences of his actions can direct himself toward divorce *or* reconciliation.

Alan Leo once said '. . . in consulting astrologers, people commonly expect to be told what will happen, what they will do or what will be done to them; they seldom come in order to learn how to use their own powers of initiative more wisely . . .'

Astrology is about the unfolding of time, the unfolding of the individual psyche and not necessarily about specific predicted dates and events.

Nevertheless, there is an abundance of well known people whose natal horoscopes are worth exploring and which help clarify specific astrological indications and conditions.

None are more interesting and subject to more speculation that the horoscopes for the Royal Family. Even a cursory look at this collection of horoscopes shows that the period beginning in 1990 and continuing through into 1995 would represent a time of fundamental 'struggle' for the Monarchy, resulting in obvious damage to the reputation and, some may say, 'honour' of the Royal Family.

I write this in early 1993 yet it continues to be obvious that this period of struggle is yet to culminate. We can expect further problems within the Monarchy as there are significant astrological indications yet to complete their particular course across the charts of the Royal Family.

In the opinion of Brian and me significant events have yet to occur that will change the course of our Monarchy and November 1993 may be a particularly stressful month.

This is not the first time that His Royal Highness Prince Charles' chart has been examined and surely it will not be the last. Prince Charles' chart is well documented elsewhere in astrological literature and its inclusion here is to offer a sample of how a chart might be approached and the sort of guidance that may be gleaned from an interpretation which endeavours to assess the deeper values.

Electric Ephermis

Radix		MC	13 18 Ari	Sun	22 26 Sco	4
------		ASC	5 12 Leo	Moon	0 26 Tau	10
PRINCE CHARLES		------	Plac ------	Mercury	6 58 Sco	4
		11.	22 57 Tau	Venus	16 24 Lib	4
Date:	14 11 1948	12.	3 53 Can	Mars	20 57 Sag	5
Time:	21 14 0 E 0	2.	22 11 Leo	Jupiter	29 54 Sag	5
Latitude:	51 32 N	3.	13 40 Vir	Saturn	5 17 Vir	2
Longitude:	0 8 W	------		Uranus	29 56 Gem R	11
		Node	3 56 Tau	10 Neptune	14 8 Lib	4
		Part ft	13 26 Cap	6 Pluto	16 34 Leo	1

Aspects: Radix/Radix Orb: 8   0   **PRINCE CHARLES**

MC	Opp	Ven	3	6	MC	Tri	Mar	7	39	MC	Opp	Nep	0	50	MC	Tri	Plu	3	16
MC	Sqr	Par	0	8	ASC	Sqr	Moo	5	0	ASC	Sqr	Mer	1	32	ASC	Sqr	Nod	1	30
Sun	Sqr	Plu	5	52	Moo	Opp	Mer	6	33	Moo	Tri	Jup	0	32	Moo	Tri	Sat	4	51
Moo	Sxt	Ura	0	30	Mer	Sxt	Sat	1	41	Mer	Tri	Ura	7	2	Ven	Sxt	Mar	4	33
Ven	Cnj	Nep	2	15	Ven	Sxt	Plu	0	10	Mar	Tri	Plu	4	23	Jup	Tri	Sat	5	23
Jup	Opp	Ura	0	2	Nep	Sxt	Plu	2	26	Nod	Tri	Sat	1	21	Par	Sqr	Ven	2	58
Par	Sqr	Nep	0	43															

PRINCE CHARLES

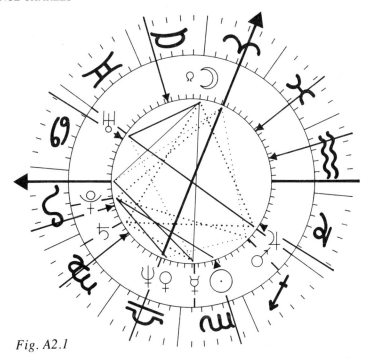

Fig. A2.1

Prince Charles's horoscope is reproduced in Fig A2.1 using the computer programme by Electric Ephemeris.

Even if there were no clues any astrologer would see, by an overview, that here was a person whose chart shows numerous beneficial aspects, i.e. specific planetary energies harmonising with one another, complimenting and benefiting the recipient. Such beneficial aspects do much to encourage a certain degree of 'ease' in life.

Consideration in any chart interpretation will include reference to the ascending or rising sign, i.e. the sign that could be seen rising on the Eastern Horizon at the moment of birth. The rising sign is of great importance and reflects the personality, the way in which the individual meets with the world. Leo the Lion, King of the Jungle, is certainly an apt rising sign for a man destined to be King for it is an Ascendant that indicates a desire for attendance, to be seen, recognised and applauded. To be centred and in control, to lead and take the stage.

However, many people are born with Leo rising and none of them – including Prince Charles so far – are kings.

Nevertheless, further inspection of his chart reveals that there are sufficient aspects between planets to provide a firm base for stating that life could certainly be successful.

Success in a public role is suggested by Prince Charles' Moon falling exalted in his Tenth House and close to a point known as the North Node. The Moon in this tenth house position will suggest a person destined for public attention who is able to present ideas and emotions to the public in empathic tones; such presentation will be sympathetically received.

When the Moon is prominent in a chart, and accentuated too in Prince Charles' by being conjunct with the Node it is likely that women (wife and/or mother) will play a significant and important 'conditioning' role. It is interesting to note too, the Queen's Sun is closely connected with Prince Charles' Moon position so the link between these two figures in the traditional, conservative and acquisitional sign of Taurus is significant. Both the Queen and Prince Charles will display determination, obstinacy and stubborn rigidity in their demands!

It is unfortunate that certain configurations involving Prince Charles' Ascendant and planet Mercury and the Moon indicate that he is capable of intense but deeply controlled irritation which may reflect itself in a tendency to speak his mind at inappropriate times and to attract criticism of his ideas and communications (despite having said earlier that his presentation will be sympathetically received). One can see how a chart interpretation can be contradictory, a criticism that many make of astrology. But is it not the nature of human beings to be contradictory?

While Charles may find himself at the centre of criticism his ideas will tend toward well thought out and well intentioned topics. He is a thinking man, reflective, a little absorptive, intense and possible deeply moved by what he senses around him. His 'communication' of his ideas may not always 'come out' quite in the way he would have liked but invariably they will be of an exciting and stimulating variety.

Whatever his irritations though, the aspects in Prince Charles's horoscope are encouraging in terms of their success and appeal as a ruler. In a configuration known as a Grand Earth Trine and involving Moon and planets Saturn and Jupiter these combine well the image of 'monarch', 'ruler' and 'king'. The Moon is often indicative of public opinion, mood, attention and the common man and is well placed in the sign of Taurus and elevated in the chart, suggesting Prince Charles to be a man of loyalty, dependability, tradition and conformity. Saturn presents authority, structure and establishment (or The Establishment!) while Jupiter indicates pomp, ceremony and opportunity. The fact that these three planets combine and relate with one another with ease and from positions of strength confirm that Charles is a man capable of succeeding in his enterprise.

Despite these obvious strengths in his chart there does exist a certain irony. Saturn strongly placed in his chart and relating to an already stable and conformist Moon indicates him to be a man of exacting standards, an extremely critical and precise man who will conform and meet his duties without fault. Jupiter, full of pomp, splendour and opportunity, while complementing these attributes, is also going to want to have fun and Charles may well find himself caught between wanting things to be precise and the desire to be free of all this exacting morality!

There is no doubt about his desire for pleasure and the enjoyment of activities that bring him a sense of vitality and which include a sporting or competitive element. Whatever his eccentricities, Charles is a man for whom a feeling of 'vitality' is a very real need. There is every indication that he is energetic, self motivated and at least willing to 'have a go' at anything that might offer a sense of freedom and excitement.

We must not forget that Charles was born with the Sun in the Fixed Water sign of Scorpio. He may present a very different persona to his Public, but within the sanctity of his home environment this Scorpio Sun is likely to show itself in a very determined, intense, even ruthless guise. Overall there is emphasis in his chart on the Fixed signs of Taurus, Leo and Scorpio, and Charles is unquestionably capable of being obstinate, stubborn and rigid.

'Fixed' means fixity in astrology and many a scenario will surely have unfolded within the portals of Buckingham Palace which confirm the pointlessness of trying to 'get through' to Prince Charles.

Some astrologers suggest that Prince Charles lacks the desire to be King. It is our opinion that Charles is an ambitious and driving man who does want the throne; the question is whether or not circumstances will allow this event to occur!

There is also a degree of the 'unknown' about Prince Charles. Planets Neptune and Venus sit close together on the nadir of the horoscope suggesting that the public image presented to the outside world is not always what he would like. These planets when together do suggest a touch of the romantic and the idealist, and all too often he will come across as a somewhat ridiculous figure. Romantically he may be inclined to lay down exacting requirements for a level of perfection quite unobtainable.

This idealistic view which we are given will disguise the Scorpio element in his chart which nevertheless exists. However quirky he may appear to be, Charles is a man of intense thought and values and his desire to achieve should never be underestimated.

Any strong Scorpio horoscope demands that the individual rise from the ashes reborn. For Charles this tendency for metaphorical rebirth may arise on his taking the throne, necessitating a fundamental change in his personal identity, i.e. a metaphorical death of the psyche. It could even lead to the transformation of the Established Monarchy and of course, this would bring about a new and irreversibly changed lifestyle for Charles. Only time will tell.

Given his tendency for 'accidents' it is interesting to observe the close aspect between planets Jupiter and Uranus. This is traditionally interpreted as 'unfortunate accidents', the luck so often associated with Jupiter being disturbed and upset by the stimulus of Uranus.

Any concluding summary of Prince Charles's chart should include the point that here is a dynamic personality.

Other points might be examined and other astrological techniques utilised. Such might reveal artistic ability, interest in the mystic, aesthetic and self-denial, discussion of and emphasis on his own ideas and thoughts and the use of his connections to advantage.

They might reveal a high, almost obsessive degree of sensitivity, an attraction to women and, surprisingly, an inclination for getting angry *very* quickly.

It might indicate a tendency to adopt any stance including that of bringing about a third person's downfall by fair means or foul, in order to get his own way.

It might reveal an ability to work vigorously for a cause, to give of himself above and beyond the normal confines of physical strength for such and perhaps to alienate entire groups of people as a result of such actions.

It might also indicate that there would be times throughout life when conditions presented themselves literally in a strict 'matter of life or death' set of circumstances.

Astrology is regrettably associated with predictive statements. If the time of birth is correct, then around 17 October 1993 and again around 17 March 1994 will be times of some sadness and dejection where the Prince and important feminine influences in his life are concerned.

There are of course, many such positions in everyone's natal chart which might be deemed stress positions – in Charles', four occur at 11° 26' of Gemini, Virgo, Sagittarius and Pisces and sometimes – but, with infuriating irregularity well known to astrologers, NOT ALWAYS! – planetary movements across or around these points will undoubtedly result in events which literally shape his life for all time.

It behoves those with even a passing interest in astrology to observe and decide whether this is so, and whether or not the results give credence to a belief that the stars sometimes influence . . . and sometimes control.

Appendix 3

Time Twins Interview Questionnaire

On the next three pages is a copy of the questionnaire which was used when interviewing the volunteers born on 14 November 1948. Only the questions listed were asked of each subject, in order to avoid any bias. The answers were written onto the form during the interview.

Under Question 2 about occupation, there are two 'supplementary' questions, asking first for the job which the subject most liked, and secondly what job the subject would have liked to have done, given the opportunity.

Under Question 3 (marriage), dates were recorded for the start and finish of each marriage if there had been more than one.

Under Question 8 (travel) it proved impracticable to list trips, and instead subjects were asked to indicate whether foreign travel had been 'extensive' or 'occasional' or 'hardly at all'.

As explained in Chapter 5, some of the questions produced no useful data. For example, none of the subjects had had any severe illness requiring confinement to hospital for more than a day or two.

It should be noted that this questionnaire is quite separate from the EPQ sent to *all* subjects earlier in the project and which was used to deduce their psychological characteristics.

TIME TWINS INTERVIEW QUESTIONNAIRE

1. NAME........................   DATE OF BIRTH............TIME....(Ind?)

2. OCCUPATION

   Jobs.....................   Dates.....................
   ....
   ....

   Preferred? ....   Desired? ....

3. MARRIAGE

   Partner's name.............   Date of marriage..............
   ....
   Children, sex.............. Born.............
   ....
   ....
   Siblings, sex............. Older/younger.................
   ....

4. ILLNESS

   Illness.................   Dates...........
   ....

   Accident...............   Dates...........
   ....

   In hospital............   Dates...........

   Caring role? ....   Dates...........

5. HOBBIES

   Hobbies/interests...
   Favourite author.............................

6. SPORT

   Sports played......................Success? ....
   Sports watched............................

7. FINANCIAL

   Event................... Date..........
   ....
   ....

8. TRAVEL

   Trip................... Date..........
   ....
   Favourite holiday...............

9. PETS

   Do you like keeping a pet? .... What sort? ....

10. SUCCESS

    What has been your greatest achievement? ....
    Date............ ....

11. FAILURE

    What has been your greatest disappointment? ....
    Date............ ....

12. INFLUENCE

    Who has been the biggest influence in your life (role model or
    parent or teacher or leader or religious figure?)
    ....

13. MUSIC

    What sort of music do you enjoy? ....

Do you play an instrument? ....

Who is your favourite composer? ....

14. ART

What sort of art do you like? ....

Do you draw or paint or make anything with your hands?

....

15. EVENTS

What have been the three most significant events in your life?

Event................   Date   ....

    ....

    ....

16. ANYTHING IMPORTANT NOT COVERED ABOVE

....

....

Appendix 4

The Gauquelin Research

Gauquelin devised a method of analysing his data and presenting it which is particularly appropriate for illustrating the nature of his findings. From a particular collection – usually a group of professionals – he would list the diurnal positions of a specific planet and then display the occurrence of the planet in each sector of the diurnal circle with the radius proportional to the planet's occurrence.

Thus, if a subject were born at 10.00 a.m. on a day when Mars had risen at 2.00 a.m. and culminated at 9.00 a.m. (for that particular geographical location) then the birth would have occurred with Mars located one hour after culmination. The interval between culmination and setting is 5 hours (from 9.00 a.m. to 2.00 p.m.) hence Mars was situated at a point on the circle $\frac{1}{5}$ of the sector between culmination and setting. If the circle is being divided into 12 then the first three sectors lie between rising and culmination, sectors 4 to 6 lie between culmination and setting and the remaining 6 fill the space between setting and rising in the lower half of the circle, below the horizon. One hour after culmination corresponds to sector 4 (sector 4 would extend from 9.00 a.m. to 10.40 a.m. because 1 hour 40 minutes is $\frac{1}{3}$ of 5 hours), and in the analysis, the total of Mars occurrences in sector 4 will be incremented by 1 as a result of including this subject. Listing of all subjects' Mars positions will yield a set of totals, one for each of the 12 sectors. To display the result, the 12 radii are made proportional in length to the sector totals.

An example of this procedure is shown below (Fig A4.1). The diagram is for Mars and 1,485 sports champions drawn from several European countries. The picture is typical of what Gauquelin found for many different collections of professionals in respect of 'appropriate planets' for each profession. There are many more occurrences of the planet, than would be

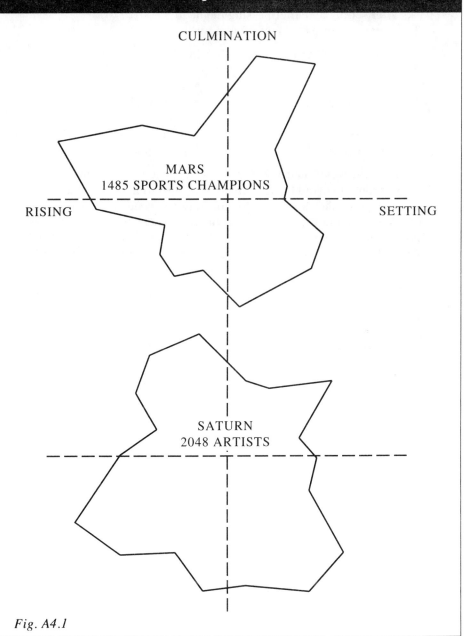

Fig. A4.1

expected by chance (highly significant statistically), immediately after rising and immediately after culmination. In addition there are two minor peaks after setting and after passing the nadir.

The same type of pattern was found for:

Professional group	Planets
Military leaders	Mars and Jupiter
Scientist and physicians	Saturn and Mars
Politicians	Jupiter and Moon
Actors	Jupiter
Writers	Jupiter and Moon

In addition, it was found that there is a tendency for a planet which is 'inappropriate' to avoid these same parts of the circle. As an example, the second diagram shows the pattern for Saturn among 2,048 painters and musicians. There are peaks in this diagram where formerly there were troughs, and vice versa.

Overall, there is a striking concordance between these findings and the traditional descriptions of planetary associations. Mars, Saturn, Jupiter and the Moon each appear prominently in the charts of those professional groups for which traditionally they could be expected. Likewise, these same planets are found to 'avoid' the key areas in those professional groups for which they are inappropriate.

Appendix 5

Analysis of Time Twins Data

This appendix contains the analysis of the time twins data. Below, and on the following 4 pages are given the original data. For each date, there is a listing in which subjects are shown line by line with the time of birth followed by the values of E, P, N and L found from answers given to the psychological questionnaire.

Occasionally, data were supplied for subjects who were born shortly before midnight on the preceding day. The time is then given as a negative number indicating how long before midnight the birth occurred. For example, someone born at 10.00 p.m. on the preceding day would be shown as -2.00. Similarly, for births occurring shortly after midnight on the chosen day, the birth time is given as a number greater than 24, e.g. someone born at 1.00 a.m. on the day after is listed as time: 25.00.

1 May 1964

Time	E	P	N	L
1.01	9	3	5	5
1.01	11	1	9	10
1.01	8	4	11	2
3.75	11	3	4	6
4.67	12	3	0	5
5.33	11	1	6	5
5.50	12	3	8	3
6.50	11	3	9	9
11.01	10	0	1	6
12.33	12	5	8	6

13.01	8	0	7	7
14.01	12	1	5	4
17.08	6	0	3	6
18.50	9	1	2	1
20.17	7	0	4	9
21.92	12	1	5	1
22.42	3	3	2	3
22.50	4	0	6	5

29 August 1958

Time	E	P	N	L
.01	3	3	7	7
.01	12	4	4	7
3.01	10	2	3	4
3.01	2	3	12	3
4.01	12	1	11	3
4.50	12	3	7	3
5.01	8	1	3	10
6.01	9	1	8	3
7.01	9	4	4	1
7.01	6	4	6	5
7.25	12	0	6	6
8.17	6	1	11	1
10.01	9	0	11	5
10.33	3	3	3	6
10.47	3	2	9	6
11.42	0	3	8	7
13.01	0	6	3	8
17.01	4	2	6	3
20.01	10	1	6	5
20.01	11	1	2	1
20.50	2	5	1	3
22.01	12	3	6	7
22.92	11	2	6	9

18 July 1950

Time	E	P	N	L
.50	3	1	10	0

1.01	12	2	2	6
1.50	2	3	11	2
4.50	2	2	4	9
5.50	6	1	9	3
6.50	8	1	8	4
8.33	12	0	10	0
8.33	9	1	11	3
12.50	5	0	5	7
13.01	0	3	12	2
19.01	8	3	11	1
20.75	8	4	9	4
21.01	2	0	12	5
21.75	12	0	1	6
22.01	1	3	2	3
22.17	12	5	3	2
23.50	10	3	0	5

14 November 1948

Time	E	P	N	L
.08	12	3	1	0
.33	3	2	8	4
.50	7	0	9	6
1.01	8	1	8	3
1.01	10	4	4	4
2.33	4	5	10	4
2.50	0	3	2	4
4.50	8	3	4	6
4.75	7	1	5	5
4.83	10	3	0	2
5.01	8	4	5	1
6.25	1	5	10	8
7.01	5	0	1	8
8.01	6	3	4	3
8.01	5	3	0	7
8.01	4	4	12	5
8.25	0	1	2	5
9.01	0	1	6	8
9.33	7	2	4	4

9.50	9	1	4	4
10.01	1	7	9	1
12.01	10	3	0	5
12.25	2	0	1	8
13.01	11	2	11	1
16.01	3	1	5	5
17.50	2	0	3	10
20.01	3	1	2	8
20.32	6	4	2	5
21.67	2	1	3	4
21.90	11	0	6	3
22.01	2	1	4	8
23.01	8	2	4	8
28.01	12	1	7	3

21 February 1937

Time	E	P	N	L
1.01	9	1	3	5
1.33	0	1	3	4
3.01	2	2	8	2
4.01	4	0	5	4
4.01	2	2	5	2
5.01	11	3	2	8
5.50	4	4	0	3
6.01	7	1	2	9
6.01	5	1	1	10
6.01	11	0	9	8
6.01	12	0	6	8
6.01	2	2	6	9
7.01	1	3	5	2
14.01	9	3	2	1
15.01	4	0	8	6
15.01	2	2	7	2
15.17	9	5	3	7
18.01	6	3	8	5
20.01	10	1	11	6
21.83	2	1	8	4
23.67	9	0	2	2

9 December 1934

Time	E	P	N	L
-.50	9	6	10	6
1.83	12	0	7	4
2.01	4	4	3	4
3.01	8	0	5	10
3.01	0	1	10	3
4.01	6	0	2	12
4.33	8	1	6	6
6.01	6	3	7	9
6.01	10	5	10	6
8.50	0	2	8	9
9.01	9	3	0	5
10.01	6	1	10	8
12.50	8	1	3	5
14.01	12	2	1	6
15.01	8	3	8	6
29.01	9	0	8	3

The 'Close Resemblers'

For 1 May 1964 there were 18 subjects. If we take the 1st with the 2nd, then the 1st with the 3rd etc. we would have 17 pairs. Then the 2nd with the 3rd, the 2nd with the 4th etc. would yield 16 pairs. Overall there would be 153 pairs. Similarly for the other 5 days. The numbers of pairs are:

Day	Sample	Pairs
1 May 1964	18	153
29 August 1958	23	253
18 July 1950	17	136
14 November 1948	33	528
21 February 1937	21	210
9 December 1934	16	120
TOTALS	128	1400

Out of the 1,400 pairs we can take those born within an hour of one another and calculate what proportion were separated by 3 units or less in

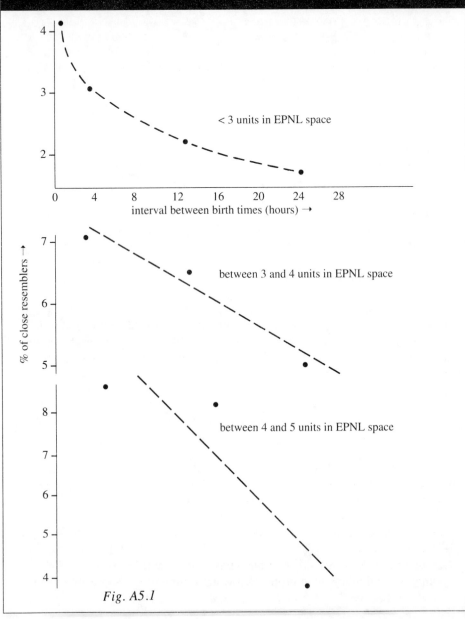

Proportions of Close Resemblers with Increasing Birth Time Interval

< 3 units in EPNL space

interval between birth times (hours) →

% of close resemblers →

between 3 and 4 units in EPNL space

between 4 and 5 units in EPNL space

Fig. A5.1

EPNL space. The proportion is 4.1% The same calculation done for pairs born at longer intervals yields proportions which fall away as the interval lengthens. Fig A5.1 shows the fall-off with time separation. At 24 hours the proportion has dropped to less than half what it is for less than 1 hour.

Even for those with less close resemblance, the fall-off can still be seen. In the other graphs are the pairs whose EPNL separation is between 3 and 4 units, and those with EPNL separation between 4 and 5 units. The overall statistical significance of each of these (independent) groups showing such a fall-off with birth time separation is about 300 to 1 against its occurring by chance.

Apart from the clear fall-off in proportions of 'close-resemblers' with increasing birth time separation, there is some tendency for pairs born on the same day to resemble one another more than if they are born on different days. In order to measure the mean separation 'between days', a random selection from one of the chosen days was paired against the same number drawn randomly from another of the chosen days, and then this same procedure repeated for all possible pairs of days (because there are 6 chosen days altogether, the number of 'day pairings' is 15). From this experiment the overall mean separation could be calculated with the following result:

Mean separation in EPNL space within days   = 7.87
Mean separation in EPNL space between days = 8.13

In fact, this difference is not statistically significant (the standard deviations of each of the two groups was about 3). However, it is of interest to note that those born on the same day do appear to resemble one another slightly more than those born on different days.

The 'resembling' effect is much more powerful for pairs who are born close together than for pairs who merely share the same day – which reinforces the other astrological research work which has been described elsewhere.

Planetary Correlations

From the answers to the psychological questionnaire we know to what extent a given subject is extrovert, neurotic etc. and from the birth time data we know where particular planets were located at the time of his or her birth. Thus a check can be carried out of any similar association to that discovered by Gauquelin. For example, we can ask if those with higher than average E values tend to have Jupiter in the cadent houses. The short answer to that question is 'no'. Only when those subjects with more extreme values of E were separated out did any pattern emerge. For the planetary correlation experiments the 'top 10%' of E values was used and similarly for the other psychological measures – the top 10% of P, N and L values.

There are 16 potential patterns obtained by trying the locations of each of the 'Gauquelin planets' – Jupiter, Mars, Saturn and the Moon – with each of the top 10% E, P, N and L. In order to make a direct comparison with the Gauquelin research, the fractions of high scoring extroverts having Jupiter in the 1st house, the 2nd house etc. all round the chart were plotted radially so that the length of a radius is proportional to the fraction of high scorers. The diagram resulting from this procedure is shown below (Fig A5.2). Similarly, the diagram for Saturn in the case of high scoring neurotics and Mars in the case of high scoring psychotics is given. Three other diagrams appear – Jupiter for high P and for high L values and Mars for high E values.

Only these 6 of the 16 potential combinations show any discernible pattern. Although the 6 yield relatively crude patterns (because they are drawn from quite small numbers of subjects) the resemblance to the Gauquelin diagrams is passable. However, one would need more than these cases to be convincing. In order to accumulate more cases and improve the signal to noise ratio, the figures from the six cases were pooled to obtain one diagram (Fig A5.3) shown below, which in itself, bears a more striking resemblance to the typical Gauquelin 'star'. In addition, those subjects lying in the lowest 10% of each of the E, P, N and L were separated and the same procedure carried out as had been employed for the top 10% cases. Now, if the Gauquelin findings are any guide, we should find the lowest 10% cases avoiding those parts of the circle where the peaks have occurred for the top 10% and, similarly, the lowest 10% cases should yield peaks where the top 10% cases have troughs. This is the acid test.

In the two diagrams below, the top 10% case has been plotted, and below it the lowest 10%. Finally, the two diagrams have been superimposed (Fig A5.4) so that the relative locations of peaks and troughs can be seen.

The result is very striking. The upper and lower 10% cases correspond to the 'preference' and 'avoidance' groups which Gauquelin identified in his work on the professions. Thus, there is good reason to suppose that his discovery of the importance of the cadent houses applies quite generally.

Planetary Patterns for the High Scorers

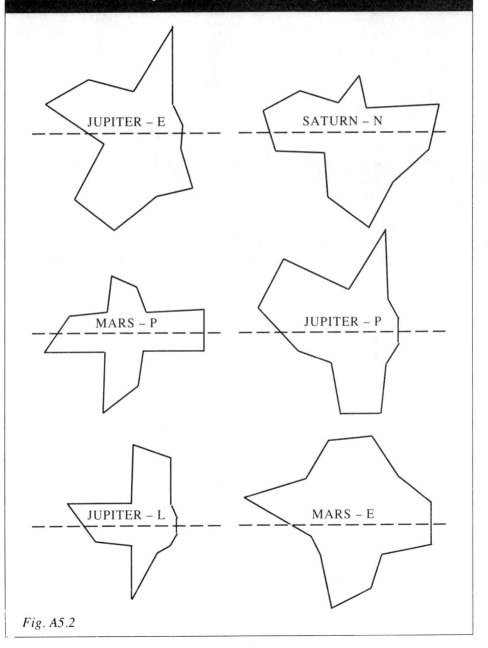

Fig. A5.2

Pooled Data – High Scorers and Low Scorers

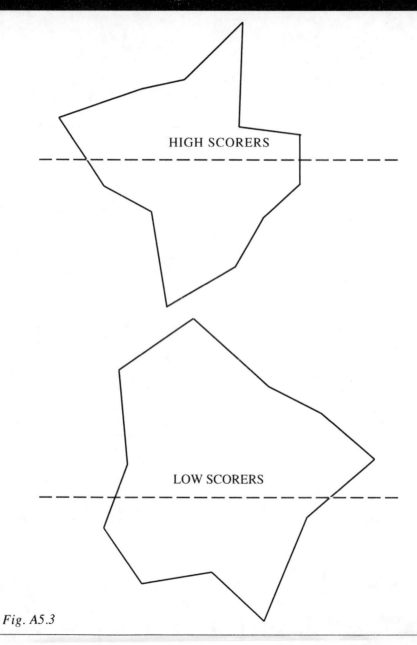

HIGH SCORERS

LOW SCORERS

Fig. A5.3

High scorers and Low Scorers compared

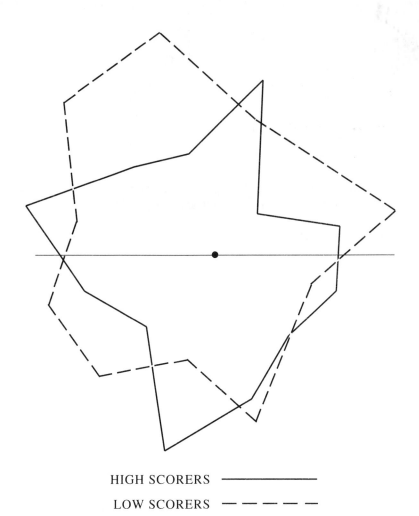

HIGH SCORERS ——————

LOW SCORERS — — — — —

Fig. A5.4

References

Chapter 1

1. 'Mirror Images Friends', *Weekly World News* (27 October 1992).
2. R. C. Smith, *Raphael's Manual Astrology* (1837).
3. A. Leo, *The Key to your Own Nativity*, Appendix.
4. G. Dean, 'Recent Advances in Natal Astrology', *Analogic* (Subiaco, W. Australia, 1977).
5. R. Harvey, *The Plantagenets* (B.T. Batsford Ltd., London 1948).
6. 'No, David Charles Heyman doesn't have a split personality', *US Magazine*.
7. R. Ebertin, 'Zwei Geburten in Der Gleichen Minute', *Kosmobiologie* (January 1969).
8. R. Ebertin, 'Combination of Stellar Influences' (COSI).

Chapter 2

1. M. Gauquelin, *The Truth about Astrology* (Hutchinson 1983).
2. V. Clark, 'Experimental Astrology', *Search* (1981).
3. M. Gauquelin, *Written in the Stars* (Aquarian Press, Wellingborough, England, 1988).
4. G. Dean, 'Recent Advances in Natal Astrology', *Analogic* (Subiaco, W. Australia, 1977).
5. M. Gauquelin, 'Planetary heredity', *ACS Publications, Inc.* (P.O. Box 16430 San Diego, CA 92116-0430 1988).
6. J.G. Toonder and J.A. West, *The Case for Astrology* (Penguin Books 1973).
7. S. Fuzeau-Braesch, 'An Empirical Study of an Astrological Hy-

pothesis in a Twin Population', *Person. indiv. Diff.* Vol 13 No 10, pp. 1135-1144 (Pergammon Press 1992).

8.   J. Mayo, O. White and H. J. Eysenck, 'An Empirical Study of the Relation between Astrological Factors and Personality', *Journal of Social Psychology* 105 (1978).

9.   J.A.H. Waterhouse, *British Journal of Social Medicine,* Vol 4 (1950).

10.   *Biologist* (Spring 1975).

Chapter 3

1.   A.H. Morrison, 'On Meeting Astrological Twins', *Astrological Review*, Vol. 44 No 3 (Winter 1972/1973).

2.   A list of astrological groups and general information can be obtained through the Urania Trust, 396 Caledonian Road, London N1 1DN.

3.   J. M. Addey, 'Selected Writings'.
       J. M. Addey, 'Astrological Twins', *Astrological Journal,* Vol IX No 1 (December 1966/1967).

4.   M. Kane, *Time Twins* (Box 1463, Murray Hill Station, New York, NY 10156-0606).

5.   T. Barneburg, 'Mothers share children's births, deaths' *Texas Express News* (San Antonio, Texas, 24 May 1989).

Chapter 4

1.   J.E. Freund, *Mathematical Statistics* (Prentice Hall Inc. Eaglewood Cliffs N. J. 1962).

2.   R. Clark, *Mail on Saturday* (7 March 1992)

3.   G. Dean, 'Recent Advances in Natal Astrology' *Analogic* (Subiaco, W. Australia 1977).

4.   M. Gauquelin, 'Planetary heredity', *ACS Publications, Inc.* (P.O. Box 16430 San Diego, CA 92116-0430 1988).

5.   B. Steffert, 'Planetary Effects Linked to EPQ Scores in Ordinary People' *Correlation*, Vol 10 No 1 (June 1990).

6.   M. Gauquelin, *Written in the Stars* (Aquarian Press, Wellingborough, England, 1988).

7.   M. Gauquelin, *The Truth about Astrology* (Hutchinson, 1983).

Chapter 5

1.   M. E. Hone, *The Modern Text Book of Astrology* (Fowler, London 1950).

Chapter 6

1.   B. Hoffman, *Albert Einstein* (Hart-Davis, MacGibbon, 1973).
2.   R. Sheldrake, *A New Science of Life* (Blond and Briggs, 1981).
3.   S. Ertel, 'Scrutinizing Gauquelin's Character Trait Hypothesis once again', *Correlation*, Vol 10, No 2 (Dec 1990).
4.   M. Gauquelin, 'Planetary heredity', *ACS Publications, Inc.* (P.O. Box 16430 San Diego, CA 92116-0430 1988).
5.   R.B. Cattell, *The Scientific Analysis of Personality* (The Chaucer Press Ltd., Bungay, Suffolk, England, 1965).
6.   D. Elwell *Cosmic Loom: The New Science of Astrology* (Unwin Hyman, London, 1987).
7.   S. Fuzeau-Braesch, 'An Empirical Study of an Astrological Hypothesis in a Twin Population', *Person. indiv. Diff.* Vol 13 No 10, pp 1135-1144, (Pergammon Press 1992).
8.   P. Seymour, *Astrology: The Evidence of Science* (Lennard Publishing, Luton, England, 1988).
9.   P. Roberts *The Message of Astrology* (The Aquarian Press, Thorsons Publishing Group, Wellingborough, England, 1990).

Appendix 1

Chart calculation services:
   Send s.a.e. to Helen Greengrass, PO Box 21, Diss, Norfolk, IP22 1PJ or enquiry to Urania Trust, 396 Caledonian Road, London N1 1DN.

Examination courses in Astrology:
   Enquire to Urania Trust (enclosing s.a.e.), 396 Caledonian Road, London N1 1DN for list of organisations offering diploma courses in astrology. Many local Adult Education Authorities run introductory classes.

Index